W9-BGX-834

Andrew B. Larkin
49 Kensington Ave.
Northampton, MA 01060

CLINICAL ETHICS,
Second Edition

ALBERT R. JONSEN, PH.D.
Professor of Ethics in Medicine,
Chief, Division of Medical Ethics
Department of Medicine, School of Medicine,
University of California, San Francisco

MARK SIEGLER, M.D.
Professor of Medicine, Department of Medicine,
Section of General Internal Medicine,
Director, Center for Clinical Medical Ethics
Pritzker School of Medicine, University of Chicago

WILLIAM J. WINSLADE, PH.D., J.D.
Professor of Preventive Medicine and Community Health
Professor of Psychiatry and Behavioral Sciences
Institute for the Medical Humanities
Director, Ethics Consultation Service
University of Texas Medical Branch at Galveston
Galveston, Texas

CLINICAL ETHICS

A Practical Approach
to Ethical Decisions
in Clinical Medicine,
Second Edition

Macmillan Publishing Company
NEW YORK

Collier Macmillan Canada, Inc.
TORONTO

Collier Macmillan Publishers
LONDON

Earlier edition, entitled *Clinical Ethics: A Practical Approach to Ethical Decisions in Clinical Medicine*
copyright © 1982
by Macmillan Publishing Co., Inc.

Macmillan Publishing Company
866 Third Avenue, New York, New York 10022

Collier Macmillan Canada, Inc.
Collier Macmillan Publishers · London

Library of Congress Cataloging-in-Publication Data

Jonsen, Albert R.
   Clinical ethics.

   Bibliography: p.
   Includes index.
1. Medical ethics.   2. Medical ethics—Case studies.
I. Siegler, Mark.   II. Winslade, William J.   III. Title.
[DNLM: 1. Ethics, Medical. W 50 J81c]
R724.J66   1986   174′.2   86–3595
ISBN 0-02-361200-2

Printing: 3 4 5 6 7 8   Year: 7 8 9 0 1 2 3 4

PREFACE

We have written this book for physicians, nurses, and medical students. We presuppose that all of our readers have some knowledge of medicine and of the clinical care of patients.

All three of us have clinical experience as either practitioners or consultants. Each of us is trained in different disciplines: Jonsen in philosophy and moral theology; Siegler in medicine; Winslade in law, philosophy, and psychoanalysis. We came away from wards and clinics, from books and lectures, with the intention of bringing our experience and training to bear on the ethical problems facing the practitioner of medicine.

Practitioners must make decisions. Thus, we do not merely discuss or analyze the ethical problems; we offer counsel about decisions. Lest this be thought presumptuous, we do not consider our counsel the single and final answer. We offer it in the tradition of medical consultation: The consultant may bring to the practitioner's view of the case not only broader information but another perspective.

Our experience with ethical problems in clinical settings, our fa-
miliarity with the literature, and our training in various fields allow us to offer broader information about certain issues than the
practitioner is likely to command. It was in the application of our
differing perspectives to each case that we grew confident enough
to offer counsel.

We are grateful to those who read our manuscript with a critical
eye: James Childress, Ph.D.; Neal Halfon, M.D.; Eugene
Hildreth, M.D.; Andrew Jameton, Ph.D; Bernard Lo, M.D.;
Henry Perkins, M.D.; Eric Jeungst, Ph.D.; Robert Nelson,
M.D.; Judy Ross, M.A.; John Robertson, J.D.; and Daniel
Wikler, Ph.D. They bear no responsibility for our faults, but
much credit for our merits. We appreciate the support of the
Henry J. Kaiser Family Foundation, the Andrew Mellon Founda-
tion, and the Walter and Elise Haas Fund.

Albert R. Jonsen
Mark Siegler
William J. Winslade

CONTENTS

LOCATOR

*Numbers refer to sections. **Boldface** numbers indicate major treatments of the topic.

CLINICAL ETHICS
Second Edition

INTRODUCTION

In routine clinical practice, physicians sometimes confront problems that are referred to as ethical problems. They appear in a variety of ways. Some are of the dramatic sort reported in the newspapers: An artificial heart is implanted in a man suffering from cardiomyopathy; a family seeks legal authority to remove a dying parent from a respirator against their physician's advice; an elderly woman refuses permission for an amputation. Others are more commonplace: How much information should be given to a fearful patient in whom cancer is detected; how should the persistently uncooperative patient be cared for; what information should be kept confidential from the family? Every physician can relate incidents of this sort, which may be described as "ethical," even though it may not be very clear as to what makes the problem an ethical one.

All practitioners face these problems from time to time; many feel distinctly uncomfortable when they do. This discomfort stems, in part, from the nature of the problems: They often involve life-and-death decisions that engage profound human emotions and

1

require intense and delicate dealings with other persons. In addition, discomfort may arise because physicians may feel they have not been trained to approach such problems systematically. Methods of analyzing and resolving ethical problems are rarely taught in medical schools. Persons whose education enables them to approach medical problems systematically and on the basis of objective data are now left with nothing more than personal intuition and common sense. Furthermore, some physicians believe that no education or method could ever improve this situation. Ethical problems, they assert, are unique; they cannot be analyzed or generalized. Each person's decision, they affirm, is that person's alone, based on personal values. Finally, some physicians may feel no discomfort at all when confronted with ethical problems; either they simply refuse to acknowledge them or they reduce them to the technical dimensions of the case.

The authors recognize the physician's discomfort with difficult ethical issues. However, this book is written with the belief that such discomfort can, to some extent, be alleviated. We identify typical situations in which ethical problems arise and illustrate ways for thinking systematically about their ethical features. We structure these problems so that their features can be clearly discerned and openly discussed. We do not solve every problem, but we do offer counsel in the form of suggestions that we believe are reasonable and practical. At best these suggestions will meet wide acceptance; at worst they will give those who disagree something definite to argue against. We admit the final decision will be made in the privacy of conscience, but we believe conscientious decisions can be made only after reviewing considerations that others have thought relevant. Thus, we provide those considerations as completely, but as briefly, as we can.

These considerations are not entirely our own. We have drawn upon the extensive literature of modern medical ethics. That literature, produced by scholars from several disciplines, has described and analyzed most of the problems we present in this book. The Reports of the President's Commission for the Study of Ethical Problems in Medicine and in Biomedical and Behavioral Research (1979–1983) are among the most valuable examples of this literature. For many issues, it is possible to discern broad consensus of opinion; for others, considerable disagreement still exists. We attempt to reflect this state of opinion in the counsel we offer.

Clinical Ethics Defined. Our book differs from others on medical ethics; it deals, more exactly, with "clinical ethics," since it concentrates on issues as they commonly arise in clinical practice. By clinical ethics, we mean the identification, analysis, and resolution of moral problems that arise in the care of a particular patient. These moral concerns are inseparable from the medical concerns about the correct diagnosis and treatment of the patient (Chapter 1). They will appear in light of the preferences patients express or do not express about their care and their future (Chapter 2). They will appear when certain sorts of futures are envisioned for that patient by others, such as physician and family (Chapter 3). They will be suggested by such matters as the costs of the patient's care and the availability of resources for proper care (Chapter 4).

The first four chapters of this book appeal primarily to those whose practice consists of adult patients. The fifth chapter treats the special problems posed by the care of infants and children. This book does not discuss the very special problems of obstetrics and reproductive medicine, although many general principles of adult and pediatric medicine apply.

This book is written not for philosophers but for practitioners who are responsible for making clinical judgments about diagnosis and treatment for their patients. Philosophers and other philosophically minded readers may be troubled by the brevity of our considerations. We are aware that our concepts, our considerations, and the counsel we offer can be further analyzed and criticized in the light of ethical theory. We have drawn on those theories, yet we refrain from theoretical analysis. We refer our readers to the *Encyclopedia of Bioethics* (EB) and to our other bibliographical citations for the deeper and broader discussion of the issues we treat so briefly. The bibliography after each chapter is generally limited to more recent articles from medical journals readily available to physician readers. The bibliography at the end of the book refers the reader to the more extensive and theoretical literature of medical ethics. (EB: ETHICS, BIOETHICS.)

The authors are also aware that some religious traditions have highly developed medical ethics. We have not drawn on these traditions to formulate substantive positions. We have, on occasion, mentioned the more prominent positions of one or another religious tradition. We suggest that physicians who do adhere to a religious faith with an explicit ethic about medicine, such as Roman Catholicism or Judaism, refer to the books cited in the bibliography that express the doctrines of those faiths. (EB: ETHICS, THEOLOGICAL; PROTESTANTISM; JUDAISM; ROMAN CATHOLICISM.)

There are brief discussions of legal matters throughout this book. These discussions are necessary because legal and ethical considerations are often mingled in clinical ethical decisions. It is useful to know the general legal concepts and something of the current legal opinion relevant to these discussions. However, this is not a book on legal medicine; anyone who needs exact legal advice should seek it from the appropriate persons and sources. We refer regularly to the helpful volume by David Meyers, *Medicolegal Implications of Death and Dying*.

HOW TO USE THIS BOOK

This book has the look of a reference work. It is arranged so that a person searching for specific information on a certain topic, say, orders not to resuscitate, can find that information quickly. However, the book has a larger purpose. It is designed to provide a method for presenting and analyzing the ethical aspects of a clinical case.

Every clinician learns from the first days of medical school to "present" a patient in an organized fashion so that diagnostic and therapeutic possibilities can be systematically explored. Similarly, this book suggests a way to "present a patient" for an ethical decision: organizing and displaying the relevant data and questions in view of reaching a practical *ethical* decision. This should help in arranging questions, gathering data, focusing on central points, excluding extraneous ones, and weighing evidence. It does not dictate conclusions. Conclusions must be drawn by the conscientious clinician after using the method to clarify and consolidate her thinking and feeling about a case.

The method for displaying the considerations involved in a clinical ethical decision consists of four general categories into which most of the considerations raised in any clinical case can be distributed. They are (1) indications for medical intervention, (2) patient preferences, (3) quality of life, (4) socioeconomic factors. A chapter is devoted to each of these categories. Each category has a twofold significance. First, it can be filled up with the actual facts, opinions, and circumstances that persons involved in the particular case are likely to bring forth. Second, each category reflects certain major moral principles and moral values that have been considered important in the ethics of medicine and health care.

Thus, the principle of beneficence plays a large role in the category devoted to indications for intervention; the principle of autonomy stands behind patient preferences; utilitarianism is influential in quality of life; and the principles of justice inform socioeconomic considerations.

When an ethical issue is to be discussed in a clinical setting, the case should be presented in terms of the four categories. First, the indications for medical intervention should be reviewed, that is, the patient's history and clinical condition relevant to diagnosis and treatment. Expectations regarding outcome should be assessed. Second, any information about the patient's preferences regarding treatment and goals should be stated and discussed. Third, in the absence of patient preferences regarding quality of life, the range and degree of the patient's future prospects should be assessed. Finally, the socioeconomic considerations, namely, the burdens and benefits that fall on parties other than the patient, should be noted. We suggest that this is the best way of presenting the ethical aspects of the case. The full scope of information and issues will be revealed in a comprehensive and orderly way. Facts that are lacking can be gathered; consultation on special points, medical or legal, can be obtained. The precise point of the case will be manifest, and often ethical issues will be more sharply formulated and solutions to problems may begin to appear.

Although this comprehensive presentation of a case is always useful, the particular problem in the case can be approached directly. For example, a Jehovah's Witness is refusing a blood transfusion. The indications for the transfusion should be reviewed; the patient preferences stated and evaluated. Then, the current opinion in ethics and law can be examined.

The Locator (the colored pages) gives immediate reference to a particular problem. This Locator contains terms that might come to mind as descriptions of the case, e.g., Jehovah's Witness, Refusal of Treatment, Transfusions, Unusual Beliefs, Religious Beliefs, Competence. The Locator will refer the reader to the appropriate sections where these matters are discussed. Since cases are complex, there is cross-referencing in the Locator and in the text. By glancing at each of these places, you should find all the relevant features of your case; you can display them, in your mind or for others, in order to assess their importance and to reach a well-reasoned and responsible decision. Thus, by sorting out facts, opinions, and circumstances raised in the actual situation into categories that also can be viewed in light of an extensive body of ethical theory, it becomes possible to evaluate those facts, opinions, and circumstances in relation to each other. An ethical judgment, like a clinical judgment, follows from a perception of the various facts, opinions, and circumstances assessed for their ethical importance in the particular situation.

Assessing the importance of facts, opinions, and circumstances in the light of ethical categories is, of course, the most perplexing task. When facts, opinions, and circumstances are meshed with our ethical categories, we call them considerations. No ethical scales exist into which considerations can be poured until "importance" shows up on a precisely calibrated gauge. Still, rough measures can be made and are made in everyday life. In this book the rough measures are established by setting the four categories in order of priority. In the encounter between patient and physician (in the ideal situation), it is the physician's duty to recommend treatment that is medically indicated; it is the patient's right to accept or refuse those recommendations in the light of personal preferences. Thus, in the priority ordering, patient preferences are the weightiest ethical category in the physician-patient encounter. However, when medical indications clearly point to a treatment that a patient refuses to authorize, questions are asked: "What is the purpose envisioned by this treatment choice? What is the patient's need? Is the patient really competent? Can the patient's need ever be so great as to override his or her preferences?" Questions of this sort will be answered by pointing to various facts and by offering opinions. These facts and opinions, in turn, will be assessed for their relative importance. This assessment may lead to the conclusion, in a particular case, that the order of priority has shifted. For example, decisions based on medical indications take priority in emergencies when the patient is incompetent.

Some clinical situations exist in which the indications for treatment are questionable and the preferences of patients unknown. When that is so, questions about quality of life or about the importance of such "socioeconomic factors" as costs or family burdens may be raised. In our ranking, neither quality-of-life choices that are not expressed as the patient's own preferences nor socioeconomic factors have great ethical weight in clinical decisions. They move toward importance only as medical indications and patient preferences become, for various reasons explained in the text, less important. Our initial ranking of the order of ethical importance is (1) patient preferences, (2) medical indications, (3) quality of life, (4) socioeconomic factors. The manner in which this initial order is shifted in particular cases so that those lower in the scale move toward greater importance is explained in the text.

Finally, a word about language. Certain words appear frequently in the text. We speak of considerations as being "relevant," "important," and "decisive." These three words express our estimation of the place a consideration takes on our scale. "Relevant" simply means a consideration has some place in the deliberations about an ethical problem: It is not ruled out of court as "inadmissible evidence." To take a crude example, the obvious poverty of a person injured in an automobile accident is *not relevant* to a decision to provide help. If a consideration is "relevant," it will have various degrees of importance. Its greater or lesser significance can sometimes be seen intuitively; at other times it must be sought by analyzing carefully the various reasons offered for or against it. For example, it is not intuitively obvious whether the request of a patient who asks to be "put out of my misery" should or should not be honored. The importance of that preference must be judged by careful analysis of the arguments pro and con active euthanasia [3.3].* Finally, an "important" consideration may emerge as "decisive" when, after careful exploration of the implications and of other values, it appears to tip the scales in favor of a particular choice. A "decisive" consideration is one that, in view of all other relevant and important considerations, carries the greatest weight. Certainly, there will be many arguments about what counts as decisive, but we believe that in many clinical situations a large measure of agreement can be reached by thoughtful review of the relevant and important considerations.

We also use the terms "permissible" and "obligatory." An action is "permissible" when, after sufficient analysis, no "decisive" consideration emerges. "Important" considerations can be offered for alternatives, and the person faced with the choice thus may not be constrained to one or another of the alternatives. When a decisive consideration does emerge in favor of one alternative, we state that, in our view, that alternative is obligatory. Thus, we propose that it is permissible to remove from a respirator a person in the persistent vegetative state. [See 3.2.] It is obligatory, we believe, to respect a competent patient's refusal of treatment (except in quite specific circumstances [2.5]).

Our success in achieving our goals will be measured by how useful and practical our handbook is for students, house officers, nurses, and practicing physicians. We hope they will become more comfortable and confident in dealing with these difficult matters. If proper attention comes to be given to the ethical problems that arise in clinical decision-making, we will have achieved our purpose. Competent and confident physicians who are willing and able to deal with clinical ethical matters when they arise will provide the best care to patients.

BIBLIOGRAPHY

Abram, M., Wolf, S. Public Involvement in Medical Ethics: A model for government action. N Engl J Med, 1984, 310:627.

Ackerman, T. What should bioethics be? J Med Philos, 1980, 5:260.

---

* Bracketed numbers within the body of the text refer the reader to appropriate sections elsewhere in the book. The first digit indicates the chapter in which the section is to be found.

American College of Physicians Ethics Manual. Ann Intern Med, 1984, 101:129, 263.

Callahan, D. The Shattuck Lecture: Contemporary Medical Ethics. N Engl J Med, 1980, 302:1228.

Chapman, C.B. On the Definition and Teaching of the Medical Ethic. N Engl J Med, 1979, 301:630.

Clouser, K.D. Medical ethics: Some uses, abuses and limitations. N Engl J Med, 1975, 293:384.

Clouser, K.D. What is medical ethics? Ann Intern Med, 1974, 80:657.

Clouser, K.D., Culver, C., Gert, B., et al. Basic curricular goals in medical ethics. N Engl J Med, 1985, 312:253.

Gillan, R. Philosophical medical ethics. Brit Med J 1985, 290:1117, 1194, 1890; 291:130, 266.

Jonsen, A. A concord in medical ethics. Ann Intern Med, 1983, 99:261.

Meyers, D. *Medicolegal Implications of Death and Dying*. San Francisco, Bancroft-Whitney, 1981.

Reports of the President's Commission for the Study of Ethical Problems in Medicine and in Biomedical Research, Washington, D.C., Government Printing Office. *Defining Death*, 1981; *Making Health Care Decisions*, 1982; *Splicing Life*, 1982; *Decisions to Forego Life Sustaining Treatment*, 1983; *Screening and Counseling for Genetic Conditions*, 1983; *Summing Up*, 1983.

Siegler, M. Clinical ethics and clinical medicine. Arch Intern Med, 1979, 139:914.

Siegler, M. A legacy of Osler: Teaching clinical ethics at the bedside. JAMA, 1978, 239:951.

1

INDICATIONS FOR MEDICAL INTERVENTION

1.0 This chapter discusses clinical judgment regarding the risks and benefits of diagnostic and therapeutic procedures insofar as these clinical judgments are related to ethical problems. It proposes three types of medical problems commonly seen by physicians. It then describes the sorts of ethical problems that might be associated with them. It discusses in detail three ethical problems in which clinical judgment is particularly important: (1) the decision to terminate inefficacious therapy for the patient who is no longer competent; (2) the decision not to resuscitate a patient in the event of cardiorespiratory arrest; and (3) the criteria for determining that a patient has died.

The ethical principle underlying much of this chapter is the principle of "beneficence," the duty of assisting others in need and avoiding harm. This principle is expressed in the history of medicine by the Hippocratic maxim: Be of benefit and do no harm. This duty of beneficence, incumbent upon all persons, is particularly weighty for physicians who have, by profession, undertaken to care for the welfare of patients. The ethical duty of physicians and the ethical importance of the contract between physician and patient are directed to fulfilling the goals of medicine. (EB: CARE, THERAPEUTIC RELATIONSHIP, PATERNALISM, CODES OF MEDICAL ETHICS.)

1.1   RESPONSIBILITIES OF THE PHYSICIAN

The physician's central responsibility is to use medical expertise to respond to the patient's requests for help in the care of his or her health by (a) diagnosing that patient's condition, (b) informing and educating the patient about the condition—including its prognosis if treated or untreated—and about the various possible treatment alternatives, (c) recommending the course of action that the physician considers the best medical approach for that individual's problem, and (d) carrying out those procedures—for example, monitoring, prescribing—that are required by the approach chosen by the patient (or, if the patient cannot choose due to incompetence, by those authorized to do so).

1.1.1   **Evaluation of Individual Patient.**   In making a recommendation about medical care, physicians will evaluate the individual patients before them in terms of (1) the seriousness of the condition in an organic sense, (2) the seriousness of the condition in the patient's eyes, (3) the need for urgent action, (4) the possible therapeutic benefits, (5) the potential risks of the intervention, (6) alternative courses of action and inaction, (7) the physical, psychological, and social impact upon the patient of all options, (8) the ability of patients to participate in their own care, and (9) all of these in light of the patient's self-understanding, self-diagnosis, fears, and hopes.

1.1.2   **Clinical Judgment.**   The process by which a physician reaches a clinical decision requires the ability to gather data, to discern relevant differences, to discard extraneous facts, to reason probabilistically, and to make the choice to take one course of action as being the best among the many possible ones. That choice can be defended as "best" not in some absolute sense but because, given the available facts and their interpretations, judicious reflection suggests it fits the actual situation more adequately than other options. Good choices about a patient's medical care require this clinical judgment, even more so do good ethical decisions.

Physicians recognize that judgments about medical indications are not wholly and purely factual. These judgments are colored by values in many respects. Interpretation of data takes place within a complex context of assumptions. Clinical judgments reflect tacit inclinations about risk avoidance, skepticism about interventions, enthusiasm for innovation, fear of death, and many other personal values. Also, values that a physician may be loath to admit may bias outwardly "objective" judgments: anxiety regarding death and disability, disdain for certain kinds of persons or life-styles, racial prejudices, repugnance for the aged or retarded. It is important to be aware of the subtle value aspects of objective medical judgments and to recognize that they may on occasion influence the clinical decision. Thus, every clinical decision is an ethical decision as well, made in the light both of facts and of values. The diagnostic process and the therapeutic options aim at "a right and good healing action taken in the interest of a particular patient" (Pellegrino, 1981, p. 211).

A clinical ethical decision must comprehend a correct perception of the medical indications (Chapter 1), an appreciation of the patient's preferences (Chapter 2), an evaluation of the patient's quality of life (Chapter 3) and an awareness of socioeconomic considerations, such as the role of the family, the costs of care, and so on (Chapter 4). Although these are treated in distinct chapters for pedagogical purposes, the physician must be able to draw them together, assess their importance, and reach a conclusion suited to a particular patient. (EB: DECISION-MAKING, MEDICAL.)

.1.3 **Goals of Medical Intervention.** Medical indications are derived from the medical facts, together with available forms of treatment, that lead the physician to judge that some intervention may or may not be useful to the patient. Usually these indications point to quite immediate goals, for example, treatment of a blood pressure (BP) of 180/115 with antihypertensive agents, or prevention of symptoms of celiac sprue by prescribing a gluten-restricted diet.

However, behind these specific goals are the broader, more fundamental goals of medicine. There is no single goal of medicine. In the encounter between patient and physician many appropriate

medical goals may be pursued simultaneously. These goals include:

(a) Restoration of health
(b) Relief of symptoms (including physical distress and psycho-
    logical suffering)
(c) Restoration of function or maintenance of compromised
    function
(d) Saving or prolonging of life
(e) Education and counseling of patients regarding their condi-
    tion and its prognosis
(f) Avoiding harm to the patient in the course of care

The simultaneous achievement of all these goals represents the
most appropriate end for the particular encounter. This can be
accomplished when a disease entity can be identified for which
specific, curative therapy is available. In general, patients and
physicians regard the identification and successful treatment of a
curable condition to be the ideal endpoint of a medical encounter.
(EB: THERAPEUTIC RELATIONSHIP.)

> EXAMPLE. A 24-year-old man has symptoms of severe head-
> ache and neck stiffness but has no other neurologic findings.
> The physician reaches a diagnosis of bacterial meningitis. In
> such a case, prompt diagnosis and treatment with a correct
> antibiotic is likely to achieve all the medical goals noted in
> 1.1.3.

1.1.4 **Partial Achievement of Medical Goals.** In many medical situations (in contrast to acute infectious illness, acute surgical problems such as appendicitis, or self-limited diseases that improve
spontaneously) the achievement of a cure, a perfect outcome in
which all the goals of medicine are realized, is less likely. For example, there is at present no definitive cure for many of the
common chronic diseases of adulthood such as coronary artery
disease, rheumatoid arthritis, chronic obstructive pulmonary disease, or diabetes mellitus. In dealing with these conditions, patients and physicians attempt to achieve partially some of the
goals of medicine, such as relief of symptoms, patient education,
retardation of functional impairment, prolongation of life, and
maintenance of patient control and dignity. In these situations, in

contrast to the curative model, tradeoffs frequently have to be made among competing goals.

> EXAMPLE.   A male patient with chronic progressive respiratory deterioration continues to smoke cigarettes despite admonitions from the physician. A tradeoff may be occurring between prolongation of life and maintenance of function and the patient's wish to remain in control of his condition and to engage in behavior from which pleasure is derived.

.1.5   **Realistic Understanding of the Goals of Treatment.**   When these goals are unclear or when previously clear goals begin to become cloudy, ethical questions are asked: What are we accomplishing? Is the expected outcome worth the effort? Will the effects of treatment be truly beneficial for the patient? In a clinical case, ethical deliberation should begin with a realistic evaluation of the goals of intervention for the patient under consideration. The assessment of which particular goals are *desired* from a medical encounter should be a determination made jointly by patient and physician after the patient has been informed by the physician as to which goals are *possible*. It is important to distinguish between the goals of medical intervention, to which this chapter is devoted, and the goals of the encounter between patient and physician, to which chapters two, three, and four are pertinent. In defining the goals of the encounter, the physicians will consider:

(a) *The nature of the disease.*   What goals are achievable for this particular patient who has this specific condition? Of course, any such determination in medicine must be expressed in probabilities rather than certainties. (This first factor will be discussed in considerable detail throughout the remainder of Chapter 1.)

(b) *The preferences of the patient.*   What are the patient's goals in this medical encounter? In many instances, the patient's goals are indistinguishable from the physician's goals. However, it must be acknowledged that for personal, psychological, social, religious, or economic reasons, the patient's goals may differ from those of the physician. (Chapter 2 will discuss patients' preferences and how they influence medical judgment.)

(c) *The values of physicians and patients.*   Although many physicians share with patients a common perspective on the ideal goals of medicine—the cure of illness—there may be less agreement between them on which of the partial goals of medicine is more or less desirable. This may be so particularly when that partial achievement leaves the patient with significant deficits, for example, continued life but with severe neurologic damage. If the patient is competent, these differing views can be discussed. When the patient is not competent, the values of the physician regarding "quality of life" must be carefully scrutinized. Furthermore, it is also possible that physicians and patients may disagree over what goals are being sought and which goal is more desirable. (This difference in values is discussed in Chapter 3.)

(d) *Social, cultural, political, and economic realities.* Any goals sought by physicians and patients are pursued within a context of social, cultural, political, and economic realities. Availability of resources, the wealth or poverty of individuals and communities, religious and cultural beliefs, and so forth will facilitate the attainment of some goals and render others impossible. (These factors will be considered at length in Chapter 4.)

1.2 THREE FORMS OF DISEASE AND THE GOALS OF MEDICINE

Physicians encounter disease in three forms. In the first, the patient suffers from an acute illness that, once diagnosed, can be readily treated and cured. In the second, the patient experiences a process that causes serious disabilities and which, while some relief can be provided, will progress despite treatment and eventually cause death. In the third, the patient suffers a chronic disease that can be effectively treated so as to relieve many of the most debilitating effects. For simplicity in reference, we designated these three disease forms by acronyms, ACURE, CARE, COPE. It is crucial to recognize that each of these forms of disease dictates different goals of intervention. The ethical aspects of the case will depend on what goals are chosen and pursued.

1.2.1 Three Forms of Disease (ACURE, CARE, COPE) and Their Relationship to Clinical Ethical Decisions.
Physicians habitually approach medical problems by attempting to determine the indications for or against medical intervention. We suggest that they should approach ethical problems in the same manner. The first point in "presenting a patient" in view of an ethical problem

should be a careful assessment of medical indications. However, that assessment will have to look beyond the probable immediate goals of any particular intervention (e.g., the likelihood that BP will be raised by vasopressors or that lungs will be cleared by an antibiotic) toward the more fundamental goals of medicine. [See 1.1.3] In some situations medical indications will be very obvious, for example, the patient is in diabetic ketoacidosis: All medical indications clearly favor immediate insulin administration and fluid repletion. In such cases the only ethical problems likely to arise would have to do with patient's preferences not to be treated, expressed previously or in a "living will," or the prospective quality of life of a particular patient (see Chapters 2 and 3). In other cases, the medical indications themselves may lie at the center of the problem, for example, should heart and lung functions be artificially maintained for a patient in the terminal stages of cancer? Should infection or cardiac arrest be treated in such a patient? Here the ethical question bears directly on the nature of the goal being sought. What are the goals of the intervention? Are they the proper goals for this patient? Will the efforts be futile? Will the effects of the efforts be a benefit to the patient?

.2.2   **The Uncertainties of Medicine.**   Clinical medicine is "a science of uncertainty and an art of probability" (Osler, 1961). Experienced physicians appreciate that the most mature expression of the clinician's skill is the ability to make consistently good decisions when faced with uncertainty. In the following discussion concerning different disease models (which we have labeled ACURE, CARE, COPE), a series of terms such as "acute," "chronic," "critical," "reversible," and "easily treatable" are employed. These terms should be understood as probability statements rather than absolute designations. Nevertheless, more often than not clinicians would agree on whether a particular case represented, for example, an acute process, a chronic process, or an acute exacerbation of a chronic process.

1.3   **THE FIRST FORM OF DISEASE: ACURE (ACUTE, CRITICAL, UNEXPECTED, RESPONSIVE, EASILY DIAGNOSED AND TREATED)**

CLINICAL EXAMPLE OF ACURE.   A 24-year-old university student comes to an emergency room (ER) with complaints of high fever, headache, stiff neck and cough. Physical examination suggests a diagnosis of meningitis and pneumonia. The student's mental status appears intact, and no focal neurologic deficits are detected. The student gives consent for a spinal fluid examination. A Gram stain of the spinal fluid reveals many gram-positive diplococci suggestive of pneumococcal meningitis. The student is informed of the diagnosis and the physician recommends admission to the hospital for antibiotic treatment.

1.3.1 **The Features of ACURE.** In ACURE cases the disease begins abruptly, is immediately life-threatening, is unanticipated, and is caused by factors beyond the patient's control. Further, diagnostic uncertainty is minimal; treatment is relatively easy, standardized, and effective; and without treatment the possibility of death or permanent disability is great. Each term in the ACURE model requires some description and explanation:

(a) *Acute.* Acute disease is contrasted with chronic disease. An acute disease is one that unfolds in a short time (minutes or hours or days, in contrast to months or years).

> EXAMPLE. Respiratory failure from anaphylaxis is an acute illness whereas recurring bronchitis and obstructive pulmonary disease represent a chronic process.

(b) *Critical.* "Critical" is a prognostic term specifying diseases that are immediately life-threatening (in contrast to slowly progressive diseases) or that will cause immediate, serious, and irreversible functional disabilities in addition to whatever symptoms they may cause.

> EXAMPLE. Respiratory failure is a critical disease, while progressive respiratory insufficiency with functional impairment and chronic biochemical abnormalities represents a serious symptomatic illness that is not immediately critical.

(c) *Unexpected.* Unexpected diseases are those that are not anticipated by either the patient or the physician. They are contrasted with an inevitable crisis that will occur in the course of chronic or terminal diseases.

> EXAMPLE. A patient who experiences a first anaphylactic reaction to penicillin, that results in respiratory failure, has an

unexpected disease. By contrast, an episode of acute respiratory decompensation that occurs in someone with severe chronic underlying pulmonary disease would not be unexpected.

(d) *Reversible.* This concept designates the ability to alter the natural history of a disease by intervening with definitive, effective therapy (in contrast to palliative or symptomatic relief), thereby restoring the individual to the level of health and functioning enjoyed prior to the onset of this illness. *Terminal* illness is the opposite of reversible illness. Terminal illness may be acute or chronic: it is by definition *critical*; but also, by definition, specific therapy is not available to prevent functional deterioration or to save the patient's life. Palliative therapy to relieve symptoms or to prolong life is often available.

> EXAMPLE.   Respiratory failure resulting from an anaphylactic reaction to penicillin should be entirely reversible if the patient is treated quickly and adequately. By contrast, respiratory failure that results from lymphangitic dissemination of an untreatable neoplasm is not reversible, although palliative therapy may be available to temporarily relieve some symptoms.

(e) *Easily treated and diagnosed.*   Some diseases are simple to diagnose and treat. In such conditions standardized, conventional, often "one-shot" therapy, such as an operation, short-term use of a respirator, or a course of medication (such as antibiotics) can eliminate the critical condition.

> EXAMPLE.   Ventilator support in respiratory failure from penicillin anaphylaxis should be contrasted with long-term treatment such as chronic ventilator therapy for end-stage pulmonary disease. The simple, easy treatments must be distinguished from long-term discomforting therapies such as cancer chemotherapy, burn management, and chronic renal dialysis, as well as from high-risk experimental therapy such as bone marrow transplantation and heart transplantation.

1.3.2 **Clinical Goals in ACURE.**   ACURE situations allow patients and physicians to achieve most of the goals of the medical encounter, curing disease, saving life, preserving function, relieving pain and suffering, and restoring health. Furthermore the medical indication for treatment, the wishes of the physicians to treat, and the desire of the patient usually coincide. When this is so, the situation is medically and ethically unproblematical.

1.3.3   **Clinical Ethical Problems in ACURE Situations.**   Even in seemingly straightforward situations such as the ACURE model described in 1.3, ethical problems may appear and may cause clinicians considerable difficulty. With reference to the case presented in 1.3, consider the ethical difficulties that might arise, given the following changes in the situation:

(a) The patient refuses to accept antibiotic treatment (as either an inpatient or an outpatient). The patient provides no reason for refusal. [See 2.5.]

(b) After initially refusing therapy, the patient becomes lethargic and confused. The physician is concerned about treating a patient without obtaining informed consent. The physician has been led to believe that treating people without informed consent may constitute battery. [See 2.3, 2.7.2.]

(c) The patient refuses therapy, but the patient's family demands the physician treat the patient. [See 4.2.]

(d) The patient presented in 1.3.1 was known to suffer from a life-threatening underlying disease such as uncontrolled acute myeloblastic leukemia, which had failed to respond to several previous chemotherapy regimens. [See 1.4.3–1.5.2.]

(e) The patient consented to be admitted and treated. The admitting physician tried to place the patient in the neurology/neurosurgery intensive care unit (ICU), but no beds were available in the unit. The admitting physician demanded that the resident on duty in the ICU transfer an elderly stroke victim in order to make room for the student with meningitis. [See 4.5–4.5.4.]

COMMENT.   Each of the conditions in 1.3.3 introduces an ethical question into a clinical situation otherwise ethically unproblematic. The indicated treatment would provide a benefit that corresponds to the goals of medicine. The patient would, in the ordinary course, desire that benefit. The additional complications arise from patient preferences and socioeconomic factors that will be discussed in chapters two and four. However, the first step in any analysis of an ethical problem is to be clear about the nature and goals of any medical intervention for diagnostic and therapeutic purposes. In the light of these goals, the complications introduced by the conditions in 1.3.3 can be discussed. This discussion will continue in 1.5, after we have described the second disease form, CARE.

,4   THE SECOND FORM OF DISEASE: CARE (CRITICAL, ACTIVE, RECALCITRANT, EVENTUAL)

CLINICAL EXAMPLE OF CARE.   A 34-year-old man with a 15-year history of confirmed multiple sclerosis (MS) has had several flareups of his illness, which have left him severely disabled. His initial attack consisted of numbness and weakness of his right leg and decreased visual acuity in the left eye. These signs resolved, but 2 years later he developed spasticity and weakness in his left leg. Although he was told his diagnosis and although his physician attempted on several occasions to explain the nature and course of multiple sclerosis, the patient refused to participate in such discussions. He specifically requested the physician not to inform him of his prognosis.

During the past 12 years the patient has experienced episodic but progressive physical deterioration. He developed severe spasticity in his leg. He used two canes and later a walker to ambulate but is currently confined to a wheel chair. His visual acuity has declined and he is now functionally blind in one eye and almost blind in the other. He has been unable to get a penile erection and last engaged in sexual activities 6 years ago. Five years ago he developed bladder dysfunction and has required an indwelling Foley catheter for the past 3 years. In recent years, he has required repeated admissions for the management of urinary tract problems associated with his atonic bladder and indwelling Foley catheter, and on one occasion he was treated for documented gram-negative septicemia and pyelonephritis. He has also experienced difficulty controlling his oral secretions and has had two episodes of pneumonia requiring hospitalization in recent years. He has deep decubitus ulcers and probable chronic osteomyelitis. His mental status is difficult to evaluate. He is profoundly depressed, and some observers think the depression is associated with the early development of dementia.

1.4.1 **Clinical Features of CARE.** CARE describes patients who suffer from a critical disease that has active, progressive, and deleterious effects. Such conditions are often chronic, but the CARE model also describes acute incurable illness. Such chronic and acute diseases are recalcitrant to any treatment that can either cure the disease or reverse its deleterious effects (although optimal medical care may retard such effects or alleviate symptoms). Furthermore, the probable direct outcome from the disease or its medical complications is the death of the patient. The patient is usually informed and knowledgeable about the disease and its likely course. Each term in CARE requires description and explanation:

(a) *Critical.* In 1.3.1b, we defined a critical disease as one that was immediately life-threatening or caused immediate, serious, and irreversible functional disabilities. CARE also describes patients who suffer from a critical disease with active, progressive, and deleterious effects. CARE situations include patients with diseases such as multiple sclerosis (described above in 1.4), metastatic cancer, or chronic cardiac, pulmonary, or hepatic failure.

CARE includes two forms of critical illness: (1) that which occurs as an acute exacerbation of a chronic disease and (2) that which occurs as the end stage of a chronic, progressive disease. In contrast to ACURE diseases, critical illness that develops in CARE is usually not unexpected but represents anticipated progression of the underlying disease.

EXAMPLE. The case of Mr. CARE [1.4] represents an example of acute, critical disease (a life-threatening infection) superimposed on the chronic condition of MS. However, Mr. CARE's entire course of frequent and multiple infections, which are themselves not preventable by any medical or social intervention, suggests that his entire disease state has now reached the *critical* stage. One of these multiple episodes of infection will probably prove fatal. Thus his underlying disease can be described as having reached a critical stage, and also certain acute exacerbations of the underlying disease may themselves be critical.

(b) *Active.*   Many diseases are chronic and only slowly progressive. At some point, most chronic conditions enter a stage of activity in which the disease progresses rapidly and causes symptoms, functional impairment, and eventual death. In contrast to COPE [1.8], CARE describes diseases that have entered this stage of active progression. CARE can also be used to describe certain illness (e.g., extensive burns, massive intracerebral hemorrhage, or carcinomatosis). These are invariably fatal, but they present not as chronic conditions but as acute, incurable diseases.

> EXAMPLE.   A patient with postnecrotic cirrhosis has had ascites and esophageal varices for several years. Over the course of several months, the patient develops hepatic encephalopathy, a decrease in hepatic synthetic function with prothrombin time prolongation (unresponsive to parenteral vitamin K therapy), progressive and uncontrollable ascites, and several episodes of acute esophageal bleeding. This patient's chronic progressive disease has entered the *active* phase and the disease has shifted from one managed in COPE to one that represents CARE.

(c) *Recalcitrant and eventual.*   CARE refers to disease processes that are not entirely reversible. Examples of such conditions include MS, untreatable metastatic malignancies, and the late stages of pulmonary, cardiac, or hepatic failure. At the CARE stage, the treatment of such conditions does not consist of simple, "one-shot" therapy. However, individual acute problems may respond to simple interventions such as antibiotics for an infectious complication. If therapy is available for the underlying CARE problem, it tends to be long-term and difficult, such as cancer chemotherapy or renal dialysis, or experimental, such as cardiac implantation or bone marrow transplantation.

> EXAMPLE.   The MS patient described in 1.4 will be subject to repeated infections from multiple sources—lungs, bladder, skin, and bone. Even if his physicians were, for example, to treat his osteomyelitis with antibiotics and surgery, and his decubitus ulcers with skin grafts, this therapy would improve his situation only slightly. Furthermore, they would subject the patient to the risks of general anesthesia needed to perform these several operative procedures. The patient's disease is now not only active but also recalcitrant. Death will eventually occur,

and in this instance the term "eventual" is used to describe a grim prognosis measured in months or weeks rather than in years. [See 1.6.1b.]

1.4.2 **Clinical Goals in CARE.**   In contrast to ACURE, in which most of the goals of medicine are achievable [1.1.3], in the CARE model physicians and patients must lower their clinical expectations [1.1.4]. Thus, in CARE situations cure or restoration of function may not be possible, and appropriate goals of intervention might include prolongation of life, relief of pain and suffering, maximal preservation of limited function, and enhancement of the patient's dignity and sense of control regarding his or her disease and life.

1.4.3 **CARE and Some Clinical Ethical Problems.**   As noted in section 1.2.1, the physician's first response to a patient's problem should be framed in the context of an assessment of the indications for medical intervention. *In this regard, the assignment of the patient to CARE rather than ACURE is an important step in moving toward clinical-ethical decision.* This assignment requires the establishment of a diagnosis, prognosis, and therapeutic plan. Thus, the acute exacerbations of the disease must always be viewed within the general picture of a chronic and irreversible process. This awareness should influence the physicians's judgment about the nature and achievability of goals of interventions.

In general, CARE patients who are capable of expressing a choice or who have expressed and made known their wishes in the past are more likely to influence the treatment they receive than ACURE patients. At either end of the spectrum of CARE cases— asymptomatic patients or those who are terminally ill—the preferences of the patient should be decisive in determining how much and what kind of treatment such patients receive. [See Chapter 2.]

However, CARE will often present situations in which the patient's preferences cannot be directly expressed. This may take place in the advanced stages of the chronic disease, when the patient's ability to reason and/or communicate may be disrupted by the disease or its complications. [See 2.2.] When this takes place, the judgment of the physician that medical treatment is no longer useful may become the decisive ethical consideration. "No longer useful" in this context means that medical intervention is judged not likely to attain any of the goals of medicine or that it may attain one or another of those goals that, in the absence of others, is not of independent and overriding importance. [See 1.1.3–1.1.5; 1.5.]

1.4.4   Clinical Ethical Problems in Care

(a) *Decision to withdraw life support.*   Mr. CARE, now in the advanced stages of MS and suffering many complications, is in the ICU on a respirator. He is sinking rapidly. Vital signs are BP 60/40 on dopamine; pO_2 30 on positive end-expiratory pressure (PEEP) 10 mm. Should the respirator be turned off? [See 1.5.]

(b) *Decision not to intubate.*   Mr. CARE, still living in his home, lapses into coma. He is brought to the hospital and is admitted for treatment of urinary tract infection, gram-negative septicemia, shock, and the adult respiratory distress syndrome (ARDS). Therapy is begun immediately with fluids, antibiotics, and pressor agents, but the patient's physician hesitated before intubating him and placing him on a respirator. [See 3.2.]

(c) *Orders not to resuscitate.*   Mr. CARE is placed on a respirator. He recovers from the episode of gram-negative septicemia and shock. However, probably as a result of cerebral anoxia, his mental status deteriorated further and he now has a profound dementia. After being transferred from the ICU to a regular nursing unit, his physician thinks that he should be made a "no-code" case. [See 1.6.]

(d) *Irreversible coma/brain death.*   Mr. CARE experiences a respiratory arrest on the way to the ER and probably suffers 10 minutes of cerebral anoxia before adequate ventilation is reestablished. The patient is admitted to the ICU on a respirator. The patient has been comatose since admission. Doll's eyes, corneal reflexes, and pupillary reflexes are absent. Two electroencephalograms (EEGs) show slow fluctuations with no defined rhythm. The nurses report some possible facial movements. A consulting neurologist believes the patient meets brain death criteria. One week later, despite recovery from gram-negative septicemia, the patient remains in deep coma. Physicians wonder how aggressively they should treat this patient with ARDS and whether it would be "right" to treat a new infection if it were to develop. [See 1.7.]

(e) *"Living will."* On admission, this patient's attorney contacts the physicians and informs them that the patient had executed a "living will" 5 years earlier and had updated it one year before. In this document the patient stated that, if a situation arose in which he was no longer able to speak or make decisions for himself, he absolutely did not want to be placed on a respirator, an "artificial breathing device" [2.6].

Situations (a), (b), (c), and (d) are ethical problems typical of CARE. They will be discussed at length in the following sections. Situation (e), "the living will," will be discussed in Chapter 2, Patient Preferences. Situations similar to (a), (b), and (c) that involve quality of life issues will be treated again in Chapter 3.

1.5   **DECISIONS TO TERMINATE OR WITHHOLD INTERVENTION AS MEDICALLY INEFFICACIOUS OR FUTILE**

In 1.4.4a and b Mr. CARE's situation is critical. The physician wonders about the efficacy of medical intervention: in (1) the continued use of the respirator, in (2) intubation and initiation of respirator support. Of course, the respirator will be efficacious in a certain sense, namely, gas exchange, compromised by ARDS, will be improved. This attains, in partial fashion, several of the goals of medicine: compromised function of several essential organ systems is maintained and, as a result, life is prolonged, at least for a time. However, the physician's doubts about efficacy are of a more fundamental nature: Given the presence of a lethal disease in its final stages and radical damage to multiple systems, none of medicine's other important goals will be attained. The patient certainly will not be restored to health: pain and symptoms will not be alleviated: compromised functions will not be restored or improved, but at best substituted for by mechanical means. Will further intervention be useful or efficacious in the larger sense?

(a) In 1.4.4a, given the patient's vital signs, he appears to be close to death, whether or not the respirator is continued. No medical intervention will reverse this course. If it does retard the course, clinical experience suggests it will be for several hours at best.

Further medical intervention can rightly be called *inefficacious*, that is, it will not produce the results sought. It is ethically and legally permissible to turn off the respirator.

(b) Considering the complexity of this patient's situation in 1.4.4b, the probabilities of his recovery from sepsis and ARDS are low to the vanishing point. Although return to adequate lung function is remotely possible, even if this were accomplished, clinical experience with similar patients suggests this patient is entering the terminal phase of his illness. His survival, under the best of circumstances, will probably be no more than several weeks. The patient is not likely to emerge from his comatose condition. Medical intervention, while capable of prolonging life briefly and supporting compromised function, also prolongs the terminal stage of this patient's dying. Medical intervention can rightly be called *futile*; that is, the results are temporary and fleeting and will not improve the patient's condition. Given this dubious attainment of medical goals, it is ethically permissible not to intubate.

COMMENT.   A judgment about the inefficacy or futility of treatment is the most obvious ethical justification for a decision to terminate or withhold medical intervention. There is no moral obligation to perform useless or futile actions. Thus, if none of the goals of treatment is attainable, that treatment need not be initiated or continued. In principle, all this seems clear: in practice, its application is difficult. First, many interventions are useful in the short run. For example, Mr. CARE's urinary tract infection could very probably be cleared up. It is difficult to distinguish long-run from short-run efficacy. Second, one or another of the medical goals will probably be attained, for example, prolongation of life, maintenance of function. Can we or should we rank them in importance? Third (and often very prominent in the clinical setting), there is frequently uncertainty about efficacy. It is difficult to know how long one must try some intervention before judging it inefficacious. It might also be difficult to judge whether another, yet untried, intervention might succeed when others have failed.

COUNSEL.   (a) We advise that the distinction between short-run and long-run efficacy be made explicitly and carefully. In clinical

settings there is a tendency to concentrate on short-run efficacy
and to persist in interventions that have specific and likely results
rather than to view the larger picture. For example, in 1.4.4b, an
ACURE situation is superimposed upon a CARE situation in its
advanced stages. The ready therapies appropriate to ACURE
should not be allowed to disguise the underlying and uncorrect-
able lethal process. Thus, in ethical discussion about patients of
this sort, one must distinguish explicitly between long-run efficacy and short-run efficacy.

(b) With regard to the priority in importance of medical goals, we
take the position that no general ranking of these goals is possible:
Various goals are suited to various situations, for example, restoration of health is a suitable goal for an ACURE situation: it is
not an achievable goal for CARE or Chronic, Outpatient, Palliative, Efficacious (COPE). Relief from symptoms and stabilization of compromised function are suitable goals for CARE and
COPE. *However, we do take the position that attainment of the
single goal of prolonging life when progressive and critical deterioration of major systems seems to be leading to inevitable death is
not an independent and overriding goal of medicine.* In the cases
cited above, this seems to be the only goal in view. We consider
that this goal alone does not impose on the physician a moral obligation to continue intervention. In certain situations, discussed
in Chapter 3, interventions promising only short-term and partial
efficacy may be morally permissible [see 3.2].

(c) With regard to uncertainty about efficacy, we suggest the following:

   (i) Assess the evidence, from literature and from clinical experience, and reach a conclusion of reasonable certainty, that is, a
judgment that reflects the weight of available evidence. Absolute
certainty is neither possible nor necessary in judgments of this
kind.

   (ii) Distinguish doubt about efficacy from personal trepidation
or hesitation in the face of so crucial a decision. The sensitive
practitioner is bound to experience some trepidation. Also, distinguish doubt about efficacy from doubt about the ethical propriety of the act. We maintain that doubt about ethical propriety
is dispelled by a reasonable judgment that further intervention is

not useful in attaining the important goals of medicine. This judgment justifies the ethical propriety of the act in this case.

(iii) Recognize that procrastination after the data are in, is itself a decision with ethical implications.

(iv) If genuine doubt about efficacy remains, continue to treat. Significant evidence that a good chance remains to attain important goals of medicine makes intervention obligatory until time changes the picture.

NOTE A. We have, in this entire discussion, presumed that no expression of the patient's preferences is available. If there were such expression, it must, of course, be taken into consideration. Patient preferences, indeed, may be decisive consideration, either to continue or to stop treatment. The scope of this consideration is discussed in Chapter 2.

NOTE B. All of the above remarks about Mr. CARE can be applied with suitable changes to many patients suffering from the late complications of Acquired Immune Deficiency Syndrome (AIDS).

1.5.1 **"Passive Euthanasia."** What we have described is often called "passive euthanasia." We discourage the use of this phrase; it is unclear and confusing. Similarly, the terms "omission" and "commission" shed little light. Instead of these obscure distinctions, we suggest that it is ethically appropriate to discontinue treatment because there is no duty to treat when treatment is judged useless or of minimal utility, that is, when it will attain only that goal that is not of overriding and independent importance, prolonging organic life. [See 2.6.1, 3.3.]

The principal religious denominations appear to accept this position. It is taught explicitly by the Roman Catholic Church. [See 2.6.1.] While many Jewish teachers also accept it, strict Orthodox Judaism appears to be opposed. [EB: DEATH, WESTERN RELIGIOUS THOUGHT: DEATH AND DYING, ETHICAL VIEWS; JUDAISM; RELIGIOUS DIRECTIVES IN MEDICAL ETHICS.]

1.5.2 **Legal Liability.** A decision taken in accord with the above consideration appears to be free of legal liability. Even though a person dies as the result of the action or inaction of another who is responsible for the care of that person (thus, theoretically, a homicide is committed), the duty of that responsible person to provide care is terminated by the judgment of futility or uselessness of continuing. This was the judgment in an important California case [*Barber v. Superior Court*, see 3.2.7] Legal liability, civil or criminal, could arise only when there is legitimate dispute about the facts of the case. Nevertheless, even in situations where futility of intervention is clear and no other legal issues are relevant, physicians may fear legal liability. They hesitate to decide or to record their decision and the reasons for it. We suggest that careful decision, consultation, and clear records are the best protection from liability.

1.6 ORDERS NOT TO RESUSCITATE (NO-CODE ORDERS)

In 1.4.4c Mr. CARE has recovered from the episode of gramnegative septicemia and from shock. His mental status has deteriorated and he is now profoundly demented. He is transferred from ICU to the ward, and a "no-code" order is suggested by the house officer.

Orders not to resuscitate or "no-code" refer to orders given by the attending physician or by the house officers that, if a particular patient suffers cardiac or respiratory arrest, cardiopulmonary resuscitation (CPR) should not be attempted. As a result, the patient almost inevitably will die immediately. *The ethical grounds for such an order should be the sound medical judgment that the patient's death from primary disease is imminent and that further treatment for the primary disease is futile.* The distinction between this decision and the decision to terminate or withhold therapy is that (1) the patient is now in a relatively stable state, (2) death from the primary disease is anticipated very quickly, and (3) cardiac or respiratory failure is anticipated. No-code orders may also be justified by the patient's express choice [see 2.5] or by the physician's judgment about quality of survival [see 3.2]. Frequently, however, the rationale for such an order will be the judgment of futility of further intervention.

Cardiopulmonary resuscitation is an emergency medical technique to prevent sudden and unexpected death in the life-threatening situation of cardiopulmonary arrest. The existence of a medical technique or technology does not mandate its use in every case. It is the responsibility of the physician to decide which patients should be treated with which medical techniques, and the indications and contraindications to CPR should be examined in this context. Many hospitals have explicit policies regarding no-code orders, but all policies require interpretation in the clinical setting. (See Biblio 1.6.)

1.6.1 **Indications and Contraindications for CPR.** All persons who experience unexpected cardiopulmonary arrest for any known or unknown cause and who are not known to be terminally and irreversibly ill should be resuscitated. In most hospitals, all patients are "coded" unless there is a written order to the contrary. Age, mental disease, mental retardation, and chronic disease should not be grounds for withholding CPR unless special circumstances are present. The appropriate medical circumstances are presented in the following section. Other special circumstances are discussed in 3.2.

Standards for CPR, issued by the National Conference on CPR (see Biblio 1.6) state:

> The purpose of cardiopulmonary resuscitation is the prevention of sudden, unexpected death. Cardiopulmonary resuscitation is not indicated in certain situations, such as in cases of terminal, irreversible illness where death is not unexpected.

COMMENTS. (a) *Terminal, irreversible illness, and imminent death.* Cardiopulmonary resuscitation is improper medical practice in the case of cardiopulmonary arrest that occurs as the anticipated end of a terminal illness. Cardiopulmonary resuscitation should not be used on patients who are likely to succumb to their basic disease in a short time, on patients who are dying and suffering from intractable pain, or on patients who are irreversibly comatose.

(b) *Imminence of death.* One of the central concepts in deliberating about the ethical propriety of withholding CPR is the imminence of death. The question is often asked, "How imminent?" How long before death is expected in the ordinary course of this disease?" There is no precise answer in general or in the particular case. We must heed the words of Aristotle in the first book of his *Ethics*: "Our discussion will be adequate if it has as much clearness as the subject matter admits of, for precision is not to be sought for alike in all discussion." In this vein, several comments on the notion of imminent death can be offered.

(i) Some have suggested that CPR policies be written to include a definite time for "imminent death," such as 2 weeks. Presumably, this period of time would be estimated on the basis of clinical experience with patients suffering similar diseases. This "seems more exact than the subject matter admits of," as well as improbable in light of the quite different courses of patients.

(ii) The word "imminence" not only means "near or close in time": it is etymologically derived from "threatening, menacing." Thus, even though the time element may not be exact, the perception, by physicians, nurses, family, even the patient, if capable, that the end is menacingly near is important. All humans, of course, live under threat of death but, mercifully, we do not perceive its imminence at most times. When we do, a variety of factors warn of its arrival, many of which are clinically evident. Thus, imminent death should mean not only a short time, in terms of a few days or weeks, but also the perception of the menace of death's invasion.

(iii) The imminence of death also implies that, if resuscitated, the time remaining to the patient will be filled with pain, distress, further deterioration, and another critical moment (from which, in some institutions, the patient will again be rescued). It is this prospect that refraining from CPR is intended to avoid. If the time remaining is short, the ethical justification for refraining is based upon the futility of medical treatment: The patient is resuscitated only to die. If the remaining time is estimated to be longer, the considerations relevant to quality of life should be reviewed (Chapter 3).

(iv) Certain prognostic factors suggest that, even if CPR is successful, patients may survive only a short time. The morbidity resulting from CPR itself may contribute to the patient's discomfort in their last days. This consideration may be legitimately counted as a contraindication to CPR.

COUNSEL. (a) *Terminal and irreversible conditions.* Cardiopulmonary resuscitation should be withheld from patients of the following sort who are in critical condition: patients with severe chronic disease such as cancer of the pancreas that has metastasized despite surgery and chemotherapy; patients with a progressive neurologic condition such as Jacob–Creutzfeld disease; and patients with end-stage pulmonary, cardiac, or hepatic disease that has not responded to appropriate treatment.

Similarly, patients with these acute, seemingly irreversible diseases should probably not receive CPR: myocardial infarction (MI) with cardiogenic shock unresponsive to maximal treatment, acute viral or bacterial pneumonias with unresponsive ARDS, pneumocystis carinii infection in AIDS, massive intracerebral hemorrhage, or acute liver failure unresponsive to aggressive treatment. Often, CPR is not indicated in patients who have been treated vigorously for an acute problem for weeks in an ICU and whose state deteriorates and terminates in a cardiac arrest. If the vigorous therapy in the intensive care setting has not been successful, it is unlikely that a final, pro forma pounding on the chest or administration of one or several electrical shocks will reverse the precipitous downhill course. The principal determinant of success in CPR relates to the patient's underlying disease. Thus, in such instances, even if CPR is temporarily successful, the patient is likely to arrest again unless some unexpected change occurs in the patient's underlying disease.

(b) *Uncertain situations.* There are many conditions in which physicians cannot be reasonably certain that a disease is terminal and irreversible. Many kinds of trauma, such as extensive burns or head injury, that in previous times would have been invariably fatal, can now be treated successfully. Further, a variety of life-threatening infectious illnesses, tumors (such as leukemias, lymphomas, and some carcinomas), and profound physiologic derangements (such as the ARDS) may often be managed successfully. In the face of medical uncertainty, the obligation of the physician is to treat and to preserve the patient's life. Therefore, such patients usually should be candidates for CPR.

1.6.2   Who Makes the Decisions for CPR?

(a) *The physician.*   In general, physicians must decide in view of the medical indications whether or not a patient is a candidate for CPR, that is, whether a resuscitation effort is possible and appropriate. Although various guidelines have been published, none of them substitutes for clinical judgment. When the physician determines that a patient is terminally and irreversibly ill and that no additional course of therapy (or likely medical advance) offers any reasonable expectation of remission from the terminal condition, it is appropriate to consider an order not to perform CPR on the patient.

(b) *The patient.* If the patient is competent, the patient may request that CPR not be performed. This request should be honored if it is in accord with medical indications. [See 1.6.1.] If it is not in accord with medical indications, considerations about refusal of treatment are relevant. [See 2.5.]

(c) If physicians decide the patient is not an appropriate candidate for CPR and the patient is mentally competent, the patient's permission not to resuscitate should be sought.

(d) If the patient is incapable, due to mental incapacity, to participate in this decision, the matter should be discussed with relatives. In some places, law and policy may require permission of relatives; permission of legal guardians and parents of minor children should always be obtained.

(e) It is unnecessary, offensive, and probably legally meaningless to ask the patient or family to sign some sort of "release."

1.6.3 **Documentation of the Order.** Physicians should document the decision for an order not to resuscitate and should specify the reason for this decision. The documentation in the progress notes should include the medical fact and opinion underlying the order and a summary of discussion with patient, consultant staff, and family. Dissenting views also should be noted. The physician should then write an order stating the extent and duration of the decision in the order section of the chart. Everyone concerned with the care of the patient should be informed of the order not to resuscitate. Legal advice now favors an explicit record of this order and its reasons. Naturally, the order should be reviewed at regular intervals in view of the condition of the patient and should be changed when the condition of the patient warrants it.

1.6.4 **"Slow Codes" and "Partial Codes."** The decision to refrain from CPR should be clear, definite, and communicated to all relevant parties. The so-called "slow or show code" is to be repudiated as crass dissimulation. If there is a sound reason to select among the techniques of resuscitation (partial codes), for example, to attempt chest compression and electrical defibrillation but to exclude intubation, this sound reason should be clearly noted.

1.6.5 **Interventions Other than CPR.** Orders not to resuscitate are limited to refraining from CPR. In general, they do not apply to other interventions, such as refraining from the use of antibiotics, feeding or hyperalimentation, hydration, and other measures to provide comfort to the patient. The reason for this is that cardiac arrest promises a swift and painless death to one who otherwise is certain to die more slowly and with greater discomfort. Refraining from other interventions may not have the same effect. A no-code order is consistent with maximal care in every other respect. The existence of a no-code order should in no way reduce the care and attention owed to a seriously ill patient. If other specific interventions are to be discontinued, this should be specifically noted and an overall management plan devised and communicated.

> EXAMPLE.   Karen Ann Quinlan was removed from the respirator when it was decided she would not return to "a cognitve and sapient state." She then began to breathe spontaneously. The question was raised whether a no-code order should be written, then whether infections should be treated and feedings continued. It was determined to write a no-code order and not to treat infections, but to continue feeding and hydration.

COMMENT.   When it has been decided to retreat from more aggressive therapeutic efforts, physicians seem inclined to discontinue various interventions in a certain order. This order seems to be: the withdrawal of experimental therapy; the decision not to perform CPR; the discontinuation of breathing support such as respirator; the discontinuation of agents that artificially maintain BP and cardiac output; the decision not to intervene in the face of infections with antibiotic treatment; the decision to discontinue forms of alimentation such as tube feeding or parenteral hyperalimentation; and finally the decision to reduce intravenous fluids to a maintenance or even, at times, a below-maintenance level.

This stepwise retreat may appear illogical to some. They might assert that, once the imminence of death is acknowledged, efforts to forestall death should cease entirely. However, it is not so simple. First, recognition of the imminence and inevitability of death often dawns slowly. Second, the physician's investment of effort often breeds reluctance to admit defeat. Third, deep human sentiments about fighting death or providing nourishment lead to apparently illogical efforts to clear up infections or continue alimentation. Finally, physicians frequently are activists who are driven to "do something."

COUNSEL.   (a) Decisions to withdraw or withhold specific interventions should be based upon the recognition of the progressively lessening achievability of medical goals. Above all, it should reflect the deliberate decision to change from goals that are curative to forms of care that provide comfort for the dying person.

(b) Some comforting interventions also have the effect of prolonging life, for example, nutrition and hydration. Recognition of the imminence of death does not impose an *obligation* on the physician to cease all life-prolonging methods; it *permits* the physician to turn from therapy to comforting methods. [See 3.2.2.]

(c) It is important that physicians make clear to all concerned the steps to be taken and the reasons for them.

1.6.6   **Care of the Dying Patient.**   Any decision to terminate treatment or not to resuscitate should be accompanied by efforts to make the patient as comfortable as possible. The principles of Hospice care should be followed. The decision is to terminate *therapy*, that is, active interventions intended to cure or retard the course of a disease. It is not a decision to terminate *care*, i.e., medical, social, and psychological intervention to alleviate pain and to enhance the quality of the patient's last days. Above all, attention is due to relief of pain and to enhancement of abilities to interact with family and friends. The medical proverb is pertinent: Cure sometimes, relieve occasionally, comfort always. [See 3.4.]

1.7   **BRAIN DEATH**
In 1.4.4d, the question was raised whether the patient was "brain dead." This term causes much confusion. It most properly de-

scribes a patient whose heart and lungs are being activated by a respirator but whose respiratory centers in the brain stem are destroyed. Thus, if removed from the respirator, the person would not resume spontaneous breathing. The person is "dead" in the sense of lacking the intrinisic, self-generated capacity to sustain the most fundamental organic functions in an integrated manner. The language of the model legal statute regarding brain death expresses this by stating:

> An individual who has sustained either (1) irreversible cessation of circulatory and respiratory function, or (2) irreversible cessation of all functions of the entire brain, including the brain stem, is dead. A determination of death must be made in accordance with accepted medical standards. [President's Commission for Study of Ethical Problems in Medicine and Biomedical and Behavioral Research, *Defining Death*, see General References; EB: DEATH, DEFINITION AND DETERMINATION OF.]

The above is known as the Uniform Definition of Death statute and has been adopted in many jurisdictions.

1.7.1 **Differentiation of "Brain Death" and "Persistent Vegetative State."** Brain death, in the proper sense expressed above, should not be confused with the situation in which a person shows no evidence of cortical functioning, but continues to have sustained capacity for spontaneous breathing and heartbeat. This state can be called "cortical" or "cerebral" death or, more precisely, "persistent vegetative state." (American Neurological Association Criteria: see Bibliography.) The clinical signs differentiating "brain death" and "persistent vegetative state" are:

> *Brain death*. No voluntary or involuntary movement except spinal reflexes, no brain stem reflexes (e.g., apnea in presence of elevated arterial CO_2 tension when mechanical ventilation is temporarily halted, fixed and dilated pupils, no reaction to aural irrigation, abnormal doll's eyes response). Electroencephalography, which diagnoses only absence of cortical function, is not useful.

> *Persistent vegetative state*. Unresponsiveness to meaningful stimuli, decorticate posturing, visual tracking, grimacing, yawning, intact brain stem reflexes. Observation of these signs over a prolonged period (e.g., 1 to 3 months).

COUNSEL. It is ethically obligatory, in the absence of special conditions, such as preservation of organs for transplant or the presence of viable fetal life, to discontinue all medical intervention when a patient shows the clinical signs of irreversible cessation of total brain function. This patient is dead, and medical interventions, even those that support breathing, are meaningless; none of the goals of medical intervention can be accomplished.

NOTE. Some Orthodox Jewish scholars object to this position. [See Bibliography 3.2.] Also, a few other ethicists express caution, even when agreeing in principle. The question of discontinuing life support for persons who do not meet this criterion but are in persistent vegetative state raises quite different ethical issues. These are discussed in Chapter 3.

1.7.2 **Legal Issues.** Declaration of death, although usually done by a physician in accord with medical criteria, is a legal matter. Anglo-American common law sanctioned the criteria suggested by common sense and employed by doctors; the cessation of respiration and heartbeat. Many states have statutes that incorporate these criteria, and they are still commonly used by judges. In general, a physician who declares a person dead by employing the cardiopulmonary criteria, applied with due care, would be acting in accord with the law. In recent years, many states have passed "brain death statutes"; most of these statutes conform to the Uniform Definition of Death statute quoted in 1.7. These statutes do not dictate the methods whereby this cessation is determined; they should be the most reliable clinical methods available at the time. [See Bibliography, 1.7 Guidelines for the Determination of Death.] A physician who applies these criteria with due care in a state that has a brain death statute acts according to the law. (Of course, cardiopulmonary criteria may and usually will be used in most cases; their use is not abrogated by brain death statutes.) In states without brain death legislation, a physician may apply brain death criteria as widely accepted good clinical practice, but with greater uncertainty about the legal implications. Where the statute exists, presumption favors the physician in difficult legal cases about the time and cause of death, for example, when an inheritance is at issue, when an organ is removed for transplant, when criminal charges are pending against a person who attacked the decedent.

1.8   **THE THIRD FORM OF DISEASE: COPE (CHRONIC, OUTPATIENT, PALLIATIVE, EFFICACIOUS)**

CLINICAL EXAMPLE OF COPE.   A 42-year-old woman with a family history of diabetes mellitus was first noted to have diabetes 17 years ago when she presented with an episode of ketoacidosis during her first pregnancy. The pregnancy ended with a miscarriage. In the early years following her diagnosis, her diabetes was difficult to control. Although she complied with her dietary and medical regimen, she experienced frequent episodes of ketoacidosis and hypoglycemia, which necessitated repeated hospitalizations and emergency room care.

For the next 10 years, however, her diabetes was well controlled, and she required hospitalization only twice: once for ketoacidosis associated with acute pyelonephritis and once when she was admitted electively in her eighth month of pregnancy and delivered a healthy baby.

She has been actively involved in her diabetic program. She is scrupulous about her eating habits and maintains an ideal body weight. She is knowledgeable about the use of insulin and currently takes 40 Units NPH and 5 Units regular insulin each morning. On this program, her urine fractionals are negative, her fasting blood sugars are less than 100 mg% and her two-hour postprandial sugars are usually below 140 mg%. She rarely experiences episodes of hypoglycemia. Seventeen years after the onset of diabetes, she appears to have no functional impairment from her disease. However, fundoscopic examination reveals a moderate number of microaneurysms and urinalysis shows persistent proteinuria (less than 1g/day). She has no neurologic symptoms or abnormal physical findings.

.1   The Clinical Features of COPE.   We use the term "COPE" to describe ambulatory doctor–patient interactions in physicians' offices or outpatient clinics. The COPE model is the basic model for ambulatory care. In internal medicine and family practice, the ambulatory setting is where most patient–physician encounters occur. Many of these encounters are visits for checkups or for minor, self-limited illness. However, many such visits are for the care and support of patients with chronic diseases. Indeed, the majority of internists' practice is concerned with chronic diseases such as hypertension and its sequelae, heart disease and strokes; arteriosclerotic cardiovascular disease and its complications; diabetes mellitus; osteoarthritis or rheumatoid arthritis; chronic abdominal problems such as irritable bowel syndrome or peptic ulcer disease; chronic bronchitis and obstructive pulmonary disease; and cancer. Even many of the acute problems that are brought to the physician's attention are superimposed on underlying chronic diseases. These conditions represent examples of the COPE model (Chronic, Outpatient, Palliative, Efficacious).

(a) *Chronic.*   These are chronic conditions in which the patient has lived with the disease, its symptoms, and its functional impairment, often for a long time. The patient is often knowledgeable about the disease. Frequently, in the natural course of these chronic diseases, acute medical complications may develop that are related to the underlying disease.

> EXAMPLES.   Acute pulmonary edema in chronic cardiac disease or gastrointestinal hemorrhage in portal hypertension related to cirrhosis of the liver are examples of acute complications of chronic diseases.

(b) *Outpatient.*   In contrast to ACURE and CARE situations, most COPE conditions are managed in outpatient settings rather than in the hospital. This difference has important ethical implications. In the hospital, the physician and other hospital personnel have enormous power (both physical and psychological) to influence patient choices. However, in the outpatient setting, the patient is considerably more independent and powerful in interaction with physicians. In the outpatient setting, the patient's ultimate power may be wielded by simply severing contact with this particular physician or with all physicians.

(c) *Palliative.*   For most of the chronic conditions being considered in the COPE model, definitive cure does not exist, and the physician can only palliate or soften the effect of the disease. Thus, symptoms and complications may be reduced (e.g., as in diabetes) but the underlying disease is rarely modified.

(d) *Efficacious.*   Although cure is not a possibility in most COPE diseases, therapy is often effective in reducing symptoms (e.g., in rheumatoid arthritis), maintaining function (as in the diabetes example in 1.8) preserving patient dignity, and even in prolonging life (e.g., by treating chronic hypertension or chronic congestive heart failure).

1.8.2 **Medical Goals in COPE.**   In COPE situations, some of the goals of medicine are more important than others. Although preservation of life, preservation of function, and reduction in pain and suffering remain major goals, the goals of medicine may be restated in the COPE situation as follows:

(a) To use the arts of medicine, both by active intervention and, when necessary, by self-restraint, to assist the patient to live as independently and comfortably as possible.

(b) To use the art and science of medicine to minimize the patient's need for current and future medical intervention. This is done by emphasizing preventive medicine, health education and good health habits, personal responsibilities for health, and compliance with health regimens including, but not restricted to medications.

1.8.3 **Clinical Ethical Problems in Cope.**   Although the outpatient setting in which COPE situations occur is much less dramatic than the hospital setting in which ACURE and CARE predominate, the possibility of clinical ethical problems exists. Unfortunately, because these situations lack the drama of life-and-death matters, physicians and patients may fail to recognize them as ethical problems. Ethicists rarely discuss them.

COPE is defined by the achievement of a doctor–patient accommodation in which the patient chooses to seek help from a particular physician and in which the physician agrees to care for the patient. There is a unique opportunity to achieve a doctor-patient accommodation through a process of negotiation in chronic, noncritical situations. In ACURE or CARE situations, where the patient is often critically ill, negotiation and accommodation might be curtailed in order to attend to the patient's urgent medical needs. Also, the patient is clearly less capable of participating in negotiation.

The patient has greater control over COPE encounters than ACURE or CARE encounters. The patient can define a problem as one needing a doctor's help, can initiate contact with a physician (or choose not to), and at any time can change physicians or drop out of the medical system entirely.

However, the physician is also party to achieving a doctor–patient accommodation. The physician's decision to enter such an arrangement is based on (1) ability to help the patient while (2) remaining loyal to norms of behavior associated with acting responsibly as a good physician.

In COPE there is a high level of personal interaction between physician and patient; relatively frequent encounters in the office or clinic, exchange of information about the patient's progress, and discussion of matters that go beyond the illness, such as family difficulties, money problems, and so forth. In this setting, expression of preferences by the patient and by the physician play a large part. Any ethical problems encountered in COPE are likely to revolve around differences and divergencies in preferences. The next chapter explores problems of this sort, particularly:

(a) The noncompliant patient [2.8]
(b) The problem patient [2.8.1]

BIBLIOGRAPHY

1.0–1.4 *Clinical Judgment, Responsibility, Goals and Models*

Agich,G.J. (ed). *Responsibility in Health Care*. Boston, Dordrecht, and London: D. Reidel, 1982.

Beauchamp, T.L., Childress, J.F., Principles of Biomedical Ethics, 1979, Chapters 4 and 5. (See General References.)

Bosk, C.L. Occupational rituals in patient management. N Engl J Med, 1980, 303:71.

Cassell, E.J. The function of medicine. Hastings Cent Rep, 1977, 7(6):16.

Cassell, E.J. The nature of suffering and the goals of medicine. N Engl J Med, 1982, 306:639.

Cassell, E.J., Siegler, M. (eds). *Changing Values in Medicine*. Frederick, MD.: University Publications of America, 1985.

Carlton, W. "*In Our Professional Opinion . . .": The Primacy of Clinical Judgment Over Moral Choice*. Notre Dame: University of Notre Dame Press, 1978.

Churchill, L.R. Tacit components of medical ethics: Making decisions in the clinic . J Med Ethics, 1977, 3:129.

Engelhardt, H.T., Spicker, S.F., Towers, B. (eds). *Clinical Judgment: A Critical Appraisal*. Boston and Dordrecht: D. Reidel, 1977.

Gorovitz, S., MacIntyre, A. Toward a theory of medical fallability. Hastings Cent Rep, 1975, 5(6):13; J Med Philos, 1976, 1:51.

Gutheil, T., Bursztajn, H., Brodsky, A. Malpractice prevention through the sharing of uncertainty: Informed consent and therapeutic alliance. N Engl J Med, 1984, 311:49.

Jonsen, A. Do no harm. Ann Intern Med, 1978, 88:827.

Jonsen, A. Watching the doctor. N Engl J Med, 1983, 398:1531.

Kass, L.R. Ethical dilemmas in the care of the ill. JAMA, 1980, Part I, 244:1811, Part II, 244:1946.

Kass, L.R. Professing ethically. On the place of ethics in defining medicine. JAMA, 1983, 249:1305.

Kass, L.R. Regarding the end of medicine and the pursuit of health. Public Interest (Summer) 1975: 11.

Lo, B., Schroeder, S. The frequency of ethical dilemmas in medical inpatient services. Arch Intern Med, 1981, 141:1062.

Osler, Sir William, Bean, R.B., Bean, W.B. (eds). *Aphorisms From His Bedside Teachings and Writings*. Springfield: C.C. Thomas, 1961, p. 129.

Peabody, F. The care of the patient, JAMA, 1927, 88:877. Reprinted JAMA, 1984, 252:813.

Pearlman, R.A., Inui, T., Carter, W., et al. Variability in physician bioethical decision-making. Ann Intern Med, 1982, 97:420.

Pellegrino, E.D. Toward a reconstruction of medical morality: the primacy of the act of profession and the fact of illness. J Med Philo, 1979, 4:32.

Pellegrino, E.D., Thomasma, D.C.: *A Philosophical Basis of Medical Ethics*. New York: Oxford University Press, 1981.

Shelp, E. (ed). *Beneficence and Health Care*. Dordrecht, Boston and London: D. Reidel, 1982.

Winslade, W. Aggressive intervention and reluctant withdrawals: Ethical boundaries of life saving therapies. In *Neurotrauma*. M. Miner (ed). Stoneham, Mass.: Butterworth, 1986.

1.5 Decisions to Terminate or Withhold Intervention as Medically Inefficacious

Amundsen, D.W. The physician's obligation to prolong life: A medical duty without classical roots. Hastings Center Rep, 1973, 8(4):24.

Clouser, D. "The sanctity of life": An analysis of a concept. Ann Intern Med, 1973, 78:119.

Clouser, K. Allowing or causing: Another look. Ann Intern Med, 1977, 87:622.

Connery, J.R. Prolonging life: The duty and its limits. Linacr Q, 1980, 47:151.

Lo, B., Jonsen, A. Clinical decisions to limit treatment. Ann Intern Med, 1980, 93:764.

Meyers, D. *Medicolegal implications*. Chapter 8 (see General References).

Nelson, L. Primus esse utile. Yale J Biol Med, 1978, 51:655.

Optimum care for hopelessly ill patients: A Report of the Critical Care Committee of Massachusetts General Hospital. N Engl J. Med, 1976, 295:362.

Veatch, R. An ethical framework for terminal care decisions: a new classification of patients. J Am Geriat Soc, 1984, 32:665–669.

Wanzer, S., Adelstein, S., Cranford, R., et al. The physician's responsibility toward hopelessly ill patients. N Engl J. Med, 1984, 310:955.

1.6 Orders Not to Resuscitate (No-Code Orders)

Baron, C.H. The Dinnerstein Decision and 'no code' orders. N Engl J Med, 1979, 300:264.

Bedell, S., Delbanco, J., Cook, E., et al. Survival after cardiopulmonary resuscitation in the hospital. N Engl J Med, 1983, 309:569.

Bedell, S., Delblanco, J. Choices about cardiopulmonary resuscitation in the hospital: When do physicians talk to patients? N Engl J Med, 1984, 310:1089.

Evans, A.L., Brody, B. The do not resuscitate order in teaching hospitals. JAMA, 1985, 253:2236.

Lo, B., Steinbrook, R.L. Deciding whether to resuscitate. Arch Intern Med, 1983, 143:1561–1566.

Meyers, D. *Medicolegal Implications*, Chapter 9. (See General References.)

Miles, S.H., Cranford, R., Schultz, A.L. The do not resuscitate order in a teaching hospital. Ann Intern Med, 1982, 96:660.

President's Commission for the Study of Ethical Problems in Medicine and Biomedical and Behavioral Research. *Deciding to Forego Life-Sustaining Treatment* (see General References).

Rabkin, M.T., Gillerman, G., Rice, N., et al. Orders not to resuscitate. N Engl J Med, 1976, 295:364.

Standards and guidelines for cardiopulmonary resuscitation (CPR) and emergency cardiac care (ECC). JAMA, 1980, 244:453.

Wagner, A. Cardiopulmonary resuscitation in the aged: A prospective survey. N Engl J Med, 1984, 310:1129.

1.7. Brain Death

American Neurological Association Criteria. ANA Trans, 1977, 102–172.

Black, P. Brain death. N Engl J Med, 1978, Part I, 299:338; Part II, 299:394.

Cranford, R.E., Smith, H.L. Some critical distinctions between brain death and the persistent vegetative state. Ethics Sci Med, 1979, 6:199.

A Definition of irreversible coma: Report of the Ad Hoc Committee of the Harvard Medical School to Examine the Definition of Brain Death. N Engl J Med, 1968, 205:337.

Dillon, W.D., Lee, R., Tronolone, M., et al. Life support and maternal brain death during pregnancy. JAMA, 1982, 248:1089.

Guidelines for the Determination of Death: Report of the Medical Consultants on Diagnosis of Death to the President's Commission. JAMA, 1981, 246:2184.

Meyers, D. *Medicolegal Implications*, Chapter 4 (see General References.)

President's Commission for the Study of Ethical Problems in Medicine and Biomedical and Behavioral Research. *Defining Death*. (See General References.)

Veith, F., Fein, J., Tender, M., et al. Brain death: A status report of medical and ethical considerations. JAMA, 1977, 238:1744.

Youngner, S.J., Bartlett, E.T. Human death and high technology: The failure of the whole-brain formulations. Ann Intern Med, 1983, 99:252.

2

PREFERENCES OF
PATIENTS

2.0 This chapter discusses the preferences expressed by persons who seek or are in need of medical care. These preferences are always a relevant, and frequently a decisive, consideration in the ethical problems that arise in the course of care. The various issues and problems associated with the expression or the absence of preferences are discussed in the following order: (1) the ethical, legal, and psychological nature of patient preferences; (2) competence and capacity to consent or refuse; (3) informed consent and refusal of treatment; (4) the "living will"; (5) proxy consent and "presumed consent"; (6) preferences of minors; (7) the noncompliant and "difficult" patient.

The ethical principle underlying the discussions of this chapter is the principle of autonomy. This ethical principle, widely endorsed in our culture, was forcefully expressed by John Stuart Mill:

> The only part of conduct of any one for which he is amenable to society, is that which concerns others. In the part which merely concerns himself his independence is, of right, absolute. Over himself, his own

body and mind, the individual is sovereign. (*On Liberty* [1859]. New York: Appleton-Century-Crofts, 1947, p. 10.)

The principle of autonomy has a legal counterpart in the right of self-determination. In American law, the legal right to self-determination has particular import for medical care. In 1914 Justice Cardozo wrote:

Every human being of adult years and of sound mind has a right to determine what shall be done with his body. [*Schloendorff v. Society of New York Hospital.*]

The most significant ethical problem raised by the principles of autonomy and self-determination is the problem of "paternalism." Paternalism is defined as the interference with a person's liberty of action justified by reasons referring exclusively to the welfare, good, happiness, needs, interests or values of the person being coerced. Medical practice has traditionally been strongly paternalistic: Physicians have often concealed diagnoses from patients "for their own good." The ethical question is whether paternalism is ever justified and, if it is, under what circumstances. This question is discussed in the sections on truthful disclosure [2.4] and refusal of treatment [2.5].

2.1 ETHICAL, LEGAL, AND PSYCHOLOGICAL SIGNIFICANCE OF PATIENT PREFERENCES

When there are medical indications for treatment, a physician normally proposes a treatment plan, which a competent patient may either accept or refuse. *An informed, competent patient's preference to undergo or to refuse medically indicated treatment is of great ethical, legal, and psychological importance.* (EB: PATIENT'S RIGHTS MOVEMENT.)

2.1.1 **General Considerations.** Patient preferences are the legal and moral nucleus of a patient–physician relationship: In most circumstances the patient–physician relationship can be neither initiated nor sustained unless the patient desires it. Although the patient may need the assistance of a physician, it is important for physicians to remember that the patient, not the physician, has the primary legal and moral authority to establish patient–physician relationships. Patients, not physicians, are legally permitted to terminate the relationship at will; physicians who do terminate a relationship with a patient still needing help are held to certain moral and legal standards, for example, giving timely warning and even helping the patient find another physician. (See 2.10) Patient preferences are essential for competent clinical care. A physician who ignores, neglects, or disregards patient preferences when they are relevant may be violating legal, ethical, and professional expectations. (EB: THERAPEUTIC RELATIONSHIP.)

2.1.2 **Ethical Significance.** Patient preferences are ethically significant because they make explicit the values of self-determination and personal autonomy that are deeply rooted in the ethics of our culture. Autonomy is the moral right to choose and follow one's own plan of life and action. Respect for autonomy is the moral attitude that inclines one to refrain from interference with another's beliefs and actions. The recognition of patient preferences enhances the value of personal autonomy in medical care. In practice, however, many forces obstruct and limit the expression of patient preferences; such forces—the compromised competence of the patient, the informed consent process, the psychodynamics of the physician–patient interaction, the stress of illness—contribute to problems of clinical ethics considered in this chapter.

2.1.3 **Physicians' Respect for Patient Preferences.** This is essential to the development of a mature therapeutic alliance. Although patients have the legal and moral authority over physician–patient relationships, physicians have enormous power in these relationships. They can shape the course and the moral dimensions of medical care by their psychological dominance, specialized knowledge, and technical skills. The physician's power can, if misused, undermine the therapeutic relationship and destroy the fragile moral autonomy of the patient. This is not to deny that patients have important responsibilities in maintaining the relationship: still, illness and hospitalization preoccupy and even incapacitate some patients. Not all patients are equally affected by illness, but all are potentially vulnerable to a reduced level of functioning and of conscious interaction. Therefore, physicians must be particularly sensitive to the psychodynamics of patient preferences.

EXAMPLE. A 46-year-old woman with a family history of breast cancer visits her physician every 6 months for a breast examination. (Outwardly composed, she is in fact so frightened of breast cancer, from which her mother died, that she cannot bring herself to do self-examination.) On one visit the doctor notes a 2-cm mass in the left breast, and he recommends a biopsy. She refuses and abruptly terminates the visit. The physician notes in the record, "I recommended a biopsy and patient refused for unknown reason." He pursues the matter no further.

COMMENT.   This physician, despite knowing the patient's history, obviously failed to appreciate the complex dynamics of this patient's reaction to the possibility of breast cancer. Since she had visited him frequently, there was ample opportunity to explore this matter.

2.1.4   **Legal Significance.**   Patient preferences are legally significant because the Anglo-American legal system recognizes that each person has a fundamental right to control his or her own body and the right to be protected from unwanted intrusions or "unconsented touchings." An important judicial opinion states:

> Anglo-American law starts with the premises of thoroughgoing self-determination. It follows that each man is considered to be master of his own body, and he may, if he be of sound mind, prohibit the performance of life-saving surgery or other medical treatment. [*Natanson v. Kline*, 1960.]

The legal requirement of explicit consent prior to specific treatments protects patients' legal right to control what is done to their own bodies. The documentation of consent also serves as a defense for the physician against a claim that the patient's rights had been violated.

In addition, patient preferences are significant because the law has considered the patient-physician relationship to be a sort of contract. Essential to a contract is the consent of both parties. The patient–physician "contract" is sometimes described in terms of a "fiduciary relationship" in which one party is held to a higher standard of performance than in an ordinary contract. The fiduciary, in this case the physician, has an obligation to protect the best interests of the person who has entrusted himself or herself to the physician's care. Despite this obligation, the patient's consent initiates the contract and sustains it by accepting the recommendations of the physician. The patient's withdrawal of consent can terminate it.

2.1.5 **Psychological Significance.** Patient preferences are psychologically significant because the ability to express preferences and have others respect them is crucial to a sense of personal worth. The patient, already threatened by disease, has a vital need for the sense of worth and control. Furthermore, if patients' preferences are ignored or devalued, patients are likely to distrust and perhaps disregard physicians' recommendations. Patients' distrust of physicians endangers the therapeutic benefits that flow from a positive relationship. If patients are overtly or covertly uncooperative, the effectiveness of therapy is threatened. Furthermore, patient preferences are important because they may lead to the discovery of other factors—the patient's fear, fantasies, or unusual beliefs—that a physician should consider in prescribing or implementing treatment.

2.1.6 **Agreement of Preferences.** Physicians express their preferences to the patient by making recommendations regarding an appropriate course of care. Patients express their preferences to the physician by stating implicitly or explicitly their desire to be cared for, their acceptance of the physician's recommendations, and their hopes of satisfactory results. In most encounters between patients and physicians, these preferences will be in agreement: The physician will respond to the patient's preferences, and the patient will accept the physician's recommendations. In this way a therapeutic alliance that is ethically, medically, and emotionally satisfactory can be formed. However, there will be situations in which this agreement will be lacking, for example, the physician may fail to elicit the preference of the patient or may fail to provide information about which the patient can express reasonable preferences. The patient may not express preferences, may not understand information provided, or may refuse, implicitly or explicitly, the recommendations. When discord appears, ethical problems are encountered. The following sections review the most common of these problems.

2.2   COMPETENCE AND CAPACITY TO CHOOSE

Although the preferences of an informed, competent patient should be respected, how does one determine whether a patient is competent? The law presumes that adult persons are competent until proven incompetent in judicial hearing; the experience of medical practitioners, however, is that the competence of many patients is compromised, impaired, or even significantly reduced by illness, anxiety, pain, and hospitalization.

The clinician's task is complicated because the meaning of competence is unclear. Does it refer primarily to a person's *capacity* to take in information? Or does it mean that the person must *understand* information presented? How is competence related to choice? Must a competent patient only be able to choose, able to make a rational choice, or actually make a rational choice? Even if some degree of irrationality is compatible with competence, how much? Fortunately, physicians do not have to answer all these questions to show proper respect for patient preferences. Instead, the clinician must recognize how to assess for practical purposes whether a patient is competent to formulate and express preferences and whether such preferences fall within range of preferences generally comprehensible to others. If so, the preferences are decisive. If not, the physician must take additional steps to protect the interests of incompetent patients. If the physician believes that the patient's preferences are irrational, bizarre, or unintelligible, consultation with a psychiatrist or hospital administration should be sought to determine if the patient's competence should be questioned and steps taken to provide legal protection. [See Refusal of Treatment 2.5–2.5.4.]

2.2.1   **Competent Patients.**   In a clinical setting competence to consent to or refuse medical care requires at least that a person possess (1) the ability to understand and communicate the information, (2) the ability to reason and deliberate about one's choices, and (3) the ability to choose in the light of some goals and values. Hence a comatose patient is incompetent. A patient who appears to be conscious but who does not talk or communicate cannot be said to be competent unless and until communication occurs. But talking alone is insufficient; if the talking makes no sense whatsoever, a person's competence should be questioned. If the person makes sense, can carry on a relevant conversation, and formulates and expresses a preference, say, to take or not to take antibiotics, then that person's competence is not subject to challenge.

2.2.2 **Incompetent Patients.** In medical care, competence may have yet another meaning. Persons in need of medical care sometimes appear disoriented, confused, obtunded, or psychotic. The physician must determine whether they are capable of understanding their situation and making choices about it. For such situations, we prefer the terms "mental capacity" and "incapacity," describing the functioning of sensory and mental powers to process data and to draw conclusions. We use these somewhat novel terms in order to distinguish between the legal status of persons and the physician's assessment of behavior in the clinical setting. Capacity, in this sense, designates that a person can be seen to possess (1) some goals and values, (2) the ability to communicate and understand information, (3) the ability to reason and deliberate about one's choices. Incapacity means that the person is impaired in one or all of these qualities, to a greater or less degree. They cannot act as autonomous persons because they lack knowledge, understanding, or are constrained by internal or external forces from making a decision. Incapacity, in this sense refers to the patient's inability to understand or communicate information, to reason or deliberate about choices or to make choices in light of goals or values. The person is impaired in one or all of these qualities to a greater or lesser degree.

2.2.3 **Determination of Mental Capacity or Incapacity.** As a practical matter the physician should assume that an adult patient has the capacity to consent to or refuse medical care. At the same time a physician should be alert to evidence that a particular patient may lack the capacity to understand, communicate, deliberate or choose. The preliminary evidence may come from conversation with the patient, observation of the patient's behavior, or reports from third parties—staff, family members, or friends. Sometimes the patient may appear to have adequate capacity, but clues will emerge that there may be underlying emotional instability or conflict. For example, some paranoid patients appear normal until certain questions trigger a delusional belief system. It is essential to obtain as complete and accurate a history as possible to begin to assess a patient's capacity.

If a patient seems disoriented, confused, or suspicious, or is agitated, combative, and uncooperative, one naturally wonders about the patient's capacity. Unless there is plausible explanation for the behavior and unless further discussion leads to resolution of initial doubts about the patient's capacity, the physician should consider whether a consultation from a psychiatrist or psychologist is appropriate. A mental status examination, psychological evaluation, or an interview with a mental health professional might reveal latent, or confirm manifest, psychopathology. The prudent physician will assess environmental or stress factors that might cause temporary impairment of capacity in contrast to possible personality disorders.

But one must also be alert to the possibility of physical conditions known to be associated with altered mental states. Delirium and dementia may be the result of intoxication, infection, metabolic disorders, tumors, trauma, medication, or nutritional deficiencies. The suspected or confirmed presence of any of these physical conditions does not justify a judgment of incapacity in the absence of any behavioral manifestations. However, their presence does justify further investigation into the patient's capacity when unusual behavior is manifested. Also, unusual behavior should lead the physician to seek for the presence of these conditions. It is crucial to identify physical causes of altered mental states that can be reversed by medical treatment and to attempt to do so promptly.

2.2.4 **Affective State.**   The assessment of a patient's mental state may show adequate ability to process information and relatively normal emotional states. Still, a patient may exhibit certain psychological states that while not pathologic, may affect in subtle ways the ability to comprehend and choose. Anxiety and depression are often associated with illness. These can be increased almost to the point of pathology by the anticipation of surgery, unfamiliarity with hospital settings, absence of supportive family, and the like. Physicians must recognize that considerable distortion can be introduced into the relationship with patients by such reactions. It is imperative that the physician recognize these affective states and make efforts to compensate for them.

In our opinion these mental states do not constitute incapacity as such. They do indicate an impairment of good judgment. They require very special efforts at support and communication. The timing and manner of important decisions should be carefully adjusted to the patient's psychological condition so that these decisions can be made in the best possible emotional and psychological circumstances. In our opinion, physicians have a legal duty to respect the decision of persons who are not incapacitated, even though they seem depressed or anxious. However, they have an ethical duty to do everything within their power to counter the effects of depression and anxiety on the patient.

2.5 **Judgments Regarding Incapacity to Choose.** The following cases represent situations in which the question of the patient's incapacity might be raised.

> CASE I. Mr. K. M., a 38-year-old, hard-driving business executive who had multiple cardiac risk factors (smoking, borderline hypertension, obesity), awakened from sleep with substernal chest pain and shortness of breath. His wife urged him to go to the ER or to call the physician, but he refused. Several nights later he awakened with even more severe chest pain. He had great difficulty catching his breath. At his wife's urging, he went to an emergency room, where an electrocardiogram demonstrated an acute, evolving anterior wall myocardial infarction (MI). The patient was treated with low doses of morphine sulfate, and the pain resolved. As preparations were being made to admit the patient to the coronary care unit, he informed the physician he did not wish to be admitted to the hospital and was going to return to his home. His wife attempted to dissuade him from this decision. He refused to listen to her advice. The physicians at the hospital explained to the patient the risks of his returning to his home rather than being monitored in the setting of a coronary care unit and strongly urged admission. At this point, the patient showed no signs of mental illness or lack of comprehension. He had no life-threatening cardiac rhythm disturbances, and, at the time of presentation at the emergency room, he was not in left-sided heart failure. He returned home. [See 1.3–1.3.3.]

COMMENT. The ethical question is whether a crucial decision should or should not be made by someone other than the patient

for the benefit of that patient. The ethical principles of beneficence (enhancing the person's well-being) and autonomy (respect
for the person as a self-determining individual) are in apparent
conflict. The ethical choice reflects a preference for one principle
over the other.

COUNSEL.   The patient's condition is dangerous, but without a
basis for suspecting mental incapacitation the patient's refusal is
decisive. The physician may consider this a regrettable decision
but should respect it. Of course, the physician may pursue the
problem, attempting to seek reasons for the refusal, to persuade,
and to engage the help of others, such as the patient's wife. Education and vigorous persuasion constitute an ethical approach to
refusal by a person capable of choice; coercion does not.

> CASE II.   In the case presented in 1.3, Mr. ACURE has signs
> and symptoms suggestive of bacterial meningitis. He is in-
> formed of the diagnosis and told he will be admitted immedi-
> ately to the hospital for treatment with antibiotics. He abruptly
> refuses hospitalization and treatment without giving any rea-
> son. The physician explains the extreme dangers of going
> untreated and the minimal risks of treatment. The young man
> persists in his refusal. Apart from this strange adamancy, he ex-
> hibits no evidence of mental derangement or altered mental
> status. [See 1.3–1.3.3.]

COMMENT.   There is no overt clinical evidence to support a
judgment that ACURE is incapacitated. The physician might *pre-
sume* altered mental status due to fever or metabolic disturbance,
but mere presumption, in the absence of behavior, is inadequate
to justify a conclusion that Mr. ACURE is incapacitated. Nevertheless, the refusal of a treatment so necessary and entailing minimal risk, especially without offering a reason, is enigmatic. The
physician has a moral obligation to pursue the matter further. It is
important to emphasize that a refusal of treatment should not, in
and of itself, be considered the act of an incapacitated person.
Physicians will sometimes say any refusal of lifesaving treatment
is "crazy" and assume the person to be incapacitated. We believe
that in addition to the refusal there should be clinical evidence or
solid medical reason to justify the judgment of incapacity. The

ethical problem in this case may not be whether the patient is incapacitated but whether the serious medical need of a person whose capacity to choose appears intact should be treated contrary to that person's wishes. The case is further discussed and some conclusions drawn in Refusal of Treatment. [See 2.5.]

> CASE III.   T. D., a 73-year-old man, has gangrene in his left toes. Several physicians confirm the diagnosis and recommend amputation. The gangrene is not an imminent threat to his life, but the infection is slowly spreading from his toes through his foot. If an amputation is not performed, it is expected that septicemia will occur and an amputation might, at a later stage of illness, be insufficient to prevent the patient's death. [See 1.4–1.4.4.]

T. D. is oriented to time and place and his long-term memory is reliable. He has a sense of humor and engages in a coherent and reasonable conversation—except about his gangrenous foot. He knows his foot is sore and swollen, but he insists that it is getting better. Pain medication, after several weeks of severe pain without medication, may account for this belief. He is admitted to the hospital as an involuntary psychiatric patient after falling asleep while smoking and setting his couch on fire. While in the hospital, he vacillates about whether to permit an amputation. At first he consents to, and then refuses, the recommended surgery. After he is discharged, his foot gets worse. When examined by physicians, psychiatrists, and lawyers, T. D. denies he has gangrene and denies anyone told him that he had gangrene (even though he had repeatedly been told). When asked what he would do if he did have gangrene, he immediately says he would tell the doctor to amputate. A judge concludes T. D. is incompetent to refuse the needed amputation.

COMMENT.   In this case, T. D. did not accept—because of mental deficiency, psychological denial, or delusional belief—that he did in fact have gangrene and needed an amputation. Some of the important considerations that lead to a conclusion to operate contrary to the patient's expressed preferences are:

(a) T. D.'s statement that he *would* consent to amputation if he really had gangrene.

(b) T. D.'s obvious vacillation between accepting and rejecting surgery.

(c) The nature of the life-threatening illness, as opposed to some less serious disease.

(d) The relatively short time available in which to make a decision.

COUNSEL. In our opinion, the life-threatening aspects of the illness and the likelihood that death could be prevented with amputation, *along with the patient's statement that he would accept surgery if he really had gangrene*, would together constitute decisive ethical grounds to allow surgeons to proceed to amputate. This ethical conclusion leads them to seek proper legal authority.

NOTE. A crucial element in the decision was Mr. T. D.'s statement that he would accept amputation if he did have gangrene. This statement is picked out from all of Mr. T. D.'s other statements as representative of his "true" wishes—what he would wish if he did not have delusional beliefs. The physicians have seized upon this statement because it conforms to the reality they see and supports the decisions they believe reasonable. In fact, the statement itself might flow from the complex psychological process that produces the denial. This picking and choosing among a patient's statements to find the "right" one, or the assumption that certain statements mean something the physicians wish to hear, is problematic. On the one hand, it represents an honest attempt to acknowledge the patient's preferences; on the other, it comes close to a rationalization for the doctors' getting their own way. In this case, we believe the decision to be ethically correct and the assumption of Mr. T. D.'s true wishes not unreasonable. The ethical correctness, it must be noted, rests not only on this assumption but on all four factors mentioned under "Comment" taken together. However, we must note that picking and choosing can be, in some cases, an unvarnished act of medical paternalism.

CASE IV. Mrs. L. O. is a 73-year-old woman who has lived alone for the last 12 years. She is known by neighbors and by her doctor to be fiercely independent and determined. She has no signs of senile dementia nor, apart from some eccentricities, does she show any abnormal behavior. Her medical problem is the same as that presented in Case III. She adamantly refuses amputation, although she insists she is aware of the consequences and accepts them. [See 1.4–1.4.4.]

COMMENT. Mrs. L. O. cannot be considered incapacitated to make choices in her own behalf; there is no evidence to support such a judgment. On the contrary, the evidence confirms she enjoys considerable capacity. She has no delusional belief and exhibits no vacillation.

COUNSEL. After being assured that she does understand her condition and its prognosis, her physician should put aside the thought of seeking a judicial determination of incompetence. Treatment of Mrs. L. O. should be limited to appropriate medical management. Continuing efforts to persuade her to accept amputation might be made.

2.2.6 **Evaluating Capacity to Choose in Relation to the Need for Intervention.** Usually a patient's capacity is not seriously questioned unless the patient decides to refuse or discontinue treatment. In such situations tests of capacity to consent might be applied. These tests can range from the simplest tests of mental status available to any physician to the more sophisticated evaluations applied by a psychiatrist or clinical psychologists. [See 2.2.3.] It has been suggested that the stringency of the test should vary with the seriousness of the disease and urgency for treatment; the degree or level of capacity required for decision-making varies with the extent and probability of risk, with the extent and probability of benefit, *and* with consent or refusal. Thus, for example, a patient might need only a low level of capacity to *consent* to a procedure with substantial, highly probable benefits and minimal, low-probability risk, but a high level of capacity to *refuse* the same treatment. If Mr. ACURE were confused and disoriented, his consent to treatment can be accepted; his refusal should arouse suspicions of incapacity (as it did).

2.2.7 **Waxing and Waning Capacity.** Certain pathologic conditions, such as organic brain syndrome, are characterized by a movement in and out of mental clarity. A patient may be assessed as incapacitated at one time but later appear clear and oriented.

EXAMPLE. Patient CARE, with MS, is now hospitalized. In the morning he is able to converse for short periods with doctors, nurses, and his wife; in the afternoon he confabulates and is disoriented to place and time. In both conditions he expresses various preferences about his care, which are sometimes contradictory. In particular, when questioned about surgical placement of a tube to prevent aspiration, he says no in the morning and, in the afternoon, speaks confusedly and repeatedly about having the tube placed.

COUNSEL. This waxing and waning is itself the manifestation of pathology. The patient should be considered to have impaired capacity. The expression of preferences in such a state should not be considered *determinative*, unless there is consistency in the preferences expressed during periods of clarity.

2.2.8 **Unusual Beliefs.** Patients will sometimes express beliefs that appear to others as unusual and, on occasion, allow these unusual beliefs to guide their choices of medical care. Unusual beliefs are of many sorts: unsupportable claims about the physical world (e.g., the flat-earth believers), claims about health and medical treatment that are unverified (e.g., benefits of macrobiotic diet), theological beliefs of a sectarian nature that represent a minority interpretation of a broad religious tradition, as do the Jehovah's Witnesses or Christian Scientists, or that are idiosyncratic, such as a person or group maintaining God disapproves of drug therapy. Indeed, any opinions and beliefs at variance with common cultural presumptions are "unusual." Such beliefs often considered as manifestations of a disordered mind. Thus physicians and nurses may judge as crazy anyone refusing standard medical treatment. But the mere fact of adherence to an unusual belief is not in and of itself evidence of incapacity. In the absence of clinical signs of incapacity, such persons should be considered capable of choice. On occasion, however, their choices will have significant effect on their health and medical care. (For refusal of care on the grounds of unusual beliefs, e.g., the Jehovah's Witnesses' belief about blood transfusion, see 2.5.2.)

2.2.9 **Medical–Legal Decisions for Incapacitated Persons.** When a physician does have good grounds for considering a person incapacitated, what can be done legally to authorize medical treatment? There are several courses of action open to the physician, (a) If the medical treatment is not necessary to save the patient's life, the physician can honor the person's wishes and refrain from treatment in the immediate situation. Psychiatric or other forms of help might be sought. (b) If treatment is necessary to save the patient's life, the physician might proceed to treat on the basis of the legal doctrine of implied consent. [See 2.7.2.] (c) The physician might detain and treat the patient involuntarily under authorization by a particular statute in the jurisdiction. These statutes are usually quite specific, allowing the physician to treat against the patient's will only when the patient is suffering mental disease and when the patient is a danger to self or others. [See 2.7.3.] (d) The physician or some other party, such as the hospital administrator, can seek authorization to treat an incapacitated patient from the appropriate court in the jurisdiction.

In the law, competence requires mental capacities, such as understanding, reasoning, and emotional stability, sufficient to appreciate the nature and consequences of such things as making a contract or a will, standing trial, or being a parent. The degree of understanding required by the law will vary in relation to the task to be performed and the circumstances. It will be, in the last analysis, what satisfies the judge. If the person is judged "incompetent," a guardian or conservator is appointed to make decisions. The conservator may be limited to making only particular sorts of decisions, such as those concerning business affairs, for the ward. In other circumstances a conservator "of the person" is authorized to consent to medical treatment for the ward. In the legal sense then, a person may be declared incompetent in business or financial matters and yet remain legally competent to consent to or refuse medical care. Laws concerning competence, conservatorship, and guardianship vary from state to state. It should be clear that a judgment of competence or incompetence is the outcome of a specific legal process. [On Consent by Minors, see 2.7.4; 5.2.]

2.3   **INFORMED CONSENT**

Informed consent is a central element in the ethical and legal relationship between patient and physician. When making a diagnosis and recommending treatment, the physician should provide sufficient information about the patient's condition and the recommended treatment—its benefits, risks, and alternatives—to enable the patient to make a responsible decision to accept or reject the recommendations.

"Informed consent" is merely shorthand for the ethical basis of the relationship between patient and physician: an encounter characterized by "mutual participation, respect and shared decisionmaking" (President's Commission for the Study of Ethical Problems in Medical and Biomedical and Behavior Research, *Making Health Care Decisions*; See General References.). "Informed consent," then, should not designate a mechanical recitation of facts or a *pro forma* signature on a piece of paper, but rather genuine communication and agreement about the course medical care should take. This supports the values stated in 2.1: respect for personal autonomy and establishment of a reciprocal relationship.

2.3.1   **Informed Consent: Definition and Standard.**   Informed consent is defined as the willing and uncoerced acceptance of a medical intervention by a patient after adequate disclosure by the physician of the nature of the intervention, its risks, and benefits, as well as of alternatives with their risks and benefits. Disclosure is judged "adequate" by two different standards: (1) information that is commonly provided by competent practitioners in the community or the speciality; (2) information that would allow reasonable persons to make prudent choices in their own behalf. The former standard (1) allows more room for physician discretion; it is also more susceptible of being distorted by excessive paternalism. The latter standard (2) leans more on the autonomy of the patient and has been favored in many important legal decisions. A responsible practitioner would do well to use the latter (2) as the standard for disclosure.

2.3.2   **Stringency.**   The moral and legal obligation of disclosure also varies in terms of the situation; it becomes more stringent and demanding as the treatment situation moves from emergency through elective to experimental. In some emergency situations, very little information can be provided. Any attempt to inform may be at the price of precious time. Ethically and legally, information can be curtailed in emergencies. When treatment is elective, much more information should be provided. Finally, detailed and thorough information should accompany any invitation to participate in research, particularly if the research maneuver is not directed to the patient's therapy. [See 4.6.]

2.3.3   **Disclosure.**   Many studies show that persons desire information from their physicians; many practitioners are aware that their patients appreciate information. In recent years, candid disclosure, even of "bad news" has become the norm. It is widely agreed that disclosure should include:

(a) The patient's current medical status, including the likely course if no treatment is provided.
(b) The interventions that might improve prognosis, including a description of those procedures.
(c) A professional opinion about the alternatives.

In conveying this information, physicians should avoid technical terms, attempt to translate statistical data into everyday probabilities, inquire about intelligibility, and invite questions. No physician is obliged to give, as one court said, "a mini-course in medicine."

2.3.4   **Comprehension.**   The phrase "informed consent" stresses the giving of information. Most legal discussions of informed consent emphasize the amount and kind of information the doctor provides. Consent forms list risks and benefits (sometimes in excessive detail). However, the comprehension of the patient is fully as important as the providing of information.

Some studies and many anecdotes suggest that the comprehension by patients of medical information is not outstanding. At the same time studies and impressions suggest that methods of communication are poor and that little effort is made to overcome barriers to comprehension.

The physician has an ethical obligation to make reasonable efforts to assure comprehension. Explanations should be given clearly and simply; questions should be asked to assess understanding. Written instructions or printed materials should be provided. Educational programs for patients with chronic disease (COPE and CARE) should be arranged.

2.3.5   **Barriers to Communication.**   The conveying of medical information encounters many barriers. Physicians may be trapped in the technical language, troubled by uncertainty intrinsic to all medical information, worried about harming or alarming the patient, hurried and pressed by multiple obligations. Patients may be limited in understanding, inattentive and distracted, overcome by fear and anxiety. Patients may believe that decisions are the physician's prerogative; physicians may not appreciate the rationale for the patient's participation. These barriers, while high, are not insurmountable: techniques have been suggested to deal with all of them. No technique will substitute for the physician's own admission of uncertainty and willingness to share this with patients and, despite this, still to offer a sound recommendation. [See Bibliography 2.3.]

2.3.6   **Difficulties About Informed Consent.**   Many physicians feel the informed consent requirement imposes upon them an undesirable and perhaps impossible task. It is considered undesirable because adequately informing a patient takes too long and might create unnecessary anxiety. It is considered impossible because no medically uneducated and clinically inexperienced patient can truly grasp the significance of the information the physician must disclose. Even physicians, when they are patients, may not comprehend information germane to their own illness. Selective hearing because of denial, fear, or preoccupation with illnesses may account for failure to take in what one might otherwise understand. For these reasons physicians sometimes dismiss the informed consent requirement as a meaningless but bureaucratically necessary ritual.

This is a sadly limited view of the ethical purpose of informed consent. Informed consent is not merely pushing information at a patient, that would only "reinforce physician's traditional monologue of talking at and not with patients . . . it is an opportunity to enter a new and unaccustomed dialogue between physicians and their patients . . . in which both, appreciative of their respective inequalities, make a genuine effort to voice and clarify their uncertainties and then arrive at a mutually satisfactory course of action." (Katz, J. In *Genetics and the Law* (Vol. 2). A Milunsky, G.J. Annas (eds.). New York: Plenum, 1980, p. 122.) Informed consent is, in essence, shared decision making. Still, the physician is required only to make appropriate disclosures and to attempt to communicate, not to achieve the impossible. It is not legally required that physicians disclose *all* risks, for example, those of taking aspirin or of drawing blood. The physician must strive to communicate as much as is reasonably possible in a given situation.

2.3.7   **The Therapeutic Privilege.**   Difficult ethical decisions arise not only about how detailed information should be but also whether to withhold information which the physician judges might be harmful to the patient or which the patient is likely to misinterpret. The major legal decisions that have strongly stressed the duty of informed consent based upon patient autonomy have also acknowledged the so-called "therapeutic privilege." This terminology is somewhat misleading. It is not so much that physicians enjoy a special prerogative to withhold the truth. Rather, in a legal proceeding they may offer a defense to the charge of failing to inform by stating they did so "in the patient's interest."

> A disclosure need not be made beyond that required within the medical community when a doctor can prove by a preponderance of the evidence he relied upon facts which would demonstrate to a reasonable man the disclosure would have so seriously upset the patient that the patient would not have been able to dispassionately weigh the risks of refusing to undergo the recommended treatment. [*Cobbs v. Grant, 1972.*]

Another important legal decision states a caveat: The privilege does not accept the paternalistic notion that the physician may remain silent simply because divulgence might prompt the patient to forgo therapy the physician feels the patient really needs (*Canterbury v. Spence, 1972*). The justification for withholding information is discussed under "Truthful Disclosure" [2.4].

2.4   **TRUTHFUL DISCLOSURE**

Communications between physicians and patients should be truthful, that is, statements should be in accord with facts. If the facts are uncertain, that uncertainty should be acknowledged. Deception, by stating what is untrue or by omitting what is true, should be avoided. These ethical principles govern all human communication. However, in the communication between patients and physicians, certain ethical problems arise about truthfulness. Does the patient really want to know the truth? What if the truth, once known, causes harm? Might not deception help by providing hope? In the past, answers to these questions have been ambiguous. Thomas Percival's *Medical Ethics* (1802) states, ''To a patient . . . who makes enquiries, which, if faithfully answered, might prove fatal to him, it would be a gross and unfeeling wrong to reveal the truth. His right to it is suspended . . . because, its beneficial nature being reversed, it would be deeply injurious to him, to his family and to the public.'' Laypersons, on the other hand, have often expressed a different opinion. Samuel Johnson berates doctors, ''You have no business with consequences. You are to tell the truth . . . of all lying I have the greatest abhorrence of this because I believe it has been frequently practiced on myself.'' (EB: TRUTH TELLING.)

> CASE I. A 65-year-old man comes to his physician with complaints of abdominal pain that is persistent but not extreme. Studies show metastatic cancer of the pancreas. The patient has just retired from a very busy career and has made plans for a round-the-world tour with his wife. Should his diagnosis be revealed to him?

COMMENT. In recent years, commentators on this problem have moved away from the more ambiguous position of traditional medical ethics toward a strong assertion of the right of the patient to the truth. Their arguments are:

(a) There is a strong moral duty to tell the truth that is not easily overridden by speculation about possible harms.

(b) The patient has a need for the truth if he or she is to make rational decisions about actions and plans for life.

(c) Concealment of the truth is likely to undermine the patient–physician relationship. In case of serious illness, it is particularly important that this relationship be strong.

(d) Tolerance of concealment by the profession may undermine the trust that the public should have in the profession. Widespread belief that physicians are not truthful would create an atmosphere in which persons who fear being deceived would not seek needed care.

(e) Suspicion on the part of the physician that truthful disclosure would be harmful to the patient may be founded on little or no evidence. It may arise more from the physician's own uneasiness at being a "bearer of bad news" than from the patient's inability to accept the information.

(f) Recent studies have shown that the majority of patients with diagnoses of serious illness wish to know the diagnosis. This counters the presumption that patients do not want to know. Similarly, recent studies are unable to document harmful effects of full disclosure.

COUNSEL.   (a) The considerations in favor of truthful disclosure are, in our opinion, conclusive in establishing a strong ethical obligation on the physician to tell the truth to patients about their condition and its treatment.

(b) Speaking truthfully means relating the facts of the situation. This does not preclude a manner of relating the facts that is measured to perceptions of the hearer's emotional resilience and intellectual comprehension. The truth may be "brutal," but the telling of it should not be. Measured and sensitive disclosure is demanded by the ethical principle of respect for the automony of the patient. It reinforces the patient's ability to deliberate and choose; it does not overwhelm this ability.

(c) If some facts have no implications for the patient's deliberation and choices, they need not be revealed. *Example*: Liver function studies revealed that the patient with cancer of the pancreas had elevated alkaline phosphatase with normal bilirubin. Even though this suggests the development of jaundice in the future, the physician judged this information irrelevant to the patient at this time.

CASE II.   Mr. S. P., a 55-year-old teacher, has had chest pains and several fainting spells during the last 3 months. He reluctantly visits a physician at his wife's urging. He is very nervous and anxious and says to the physician at the beginning of the interview that he abhors doctors and hospitals. On physical examination, he has classic signs of tight aortic stenosis. The physician wishes to recommend cardiac catherization. However, given his impression of this patient, he is worried lest full disclosure of the risks of catheterization would lead the patient to refuse the procedure.

COMMENT.   In this case, the anticipated harm is much more specific and dangerous than the harm contemplated in the previous case. Hesitation about revealing the risks of a diagnostic or therapeutic procedure is based on the fear the patient will make a judgment detrimental to health and life. Also, in this case, there is better reason to suspect this patient will react badly to the information than the patient in Case I.

COUNSEL.   The arguments in favor of truthful disclosure apply equally to this case and to the previous one. Whether or not catheterization is accepted, the patient will need further medical care. This patient needs, above all, the benefits of a good and trusting relationship with a competent physician. Honesty is more likely to create that relationship than deception. Also, the physician's fears about the patient's refusal may be exaggerated. In addition, studies indicate that very few patients do refuse recommended procedures and that almost all patients desire disclosure. Finally, the physician might be concerned about the family's reaction if Mr. S. P. died unexpectedly during catheterization.

> CASE III.   A person who donates blood for a relative is found to be positive for HTLV III antibody. The blood is discarded and the donor's name registered as "deferred." Should he be informed?

COMMENT.   The ELIZA test is very reliable, yet a large number of false positives will appear in the general population. Also, the meaning of a positive test for the prognosis of disease is uncertain. The news can be devastating.

COUNSEL.   The donor should be informed and counselled. Since positivity suggests a risk of infectivity and there is chance that information about behavior may reduce that risk, the person has the right to this information and to education about the facts as currently known.

2.4.1   **Completeness of Disclosure.**   Disclosure of options for treatment of a patient's condition should be complete, including the options which the physician recommends and also other options which the physician may believe are less desirable but which are still medically reasonable. In so doing, the physician should make it clear why these other options are less desirable. However, it might be asked whether the obligation of truthful disclosure requires telling a patient even of those interventions that are not medically reasonable, but which a patient may wish to consider.

CASE I.   A 41-year-old woman has a breast biopsy that reveals cancer. The physician considers that the best treatment of this premenopausal woman would be a mastectomy, axillary node dissection, and perhaps adjuvant chemotherapy. Should he also describe simpler procedures that he judges less suitable for this woman, such as a lumpectomy or mastectomy without axillary node dissection?

COUNSEL.   The entire range of options should be explained with a careful delineation of the risks and benefits of each. There is no ethical prohibition against making a strong argument in favor of the option the physician considers best. Persuasion, however, should leave the patient free to choose, even if the physician believes she may choose the less effective option.

CASE II.   The same as Case I. Should the physician also reveal the existence of "unorthodox therapies," such as laetrile?

COUNSEL.   The physician is trained in the medical management of illness. The obligation to disclose extends to all those forms of management that a competent practitioner might consider reasonable in terms of the current standards of the art and science of medicine. There is no obligation to disclose the existence of interventions of any other sort. It is, however, permissible to reveal the existence of unorthodox therapies. It may be advisable to do so if the physician believes the patient may be tempted to seek these treatments. In such a case it is imperative the physician explain the risks of unorthodox treatments and strongly advise against them. (EB: ORTHODOXY IN MEDICINE.)

2.4.2   **Placebos.**   Concealing the nature of an intervention is sometimes thought to contribute to its efficacy that is, the so called placebo.

Placebo is defined as "any therapeutic procedure which is objectively without specific activity for the condition being treated" (Shapiro, 1964). This must be distinguished from the placebo effect, "the psychological, physiological, or psychophysiological effect of any medication or procedure given with therapeutic intent, which is independent of or minimally related to the pharmacologic effects of the medication or to the specific effects of the procedure and which operates through a psychological mechanism" (Shapiro, 1959). The placebo effect is known to take place as the result of many different influences: faith in the physician, administration of a medicine that the physician believes to be effective pharmacologically but is not, or actions of the physicians that are not in themselves therapeutic, such as taking a history or performing a diagnostic test. Thus, the placebo effect may take place without deliberate deception; a placebo may not be a "false" or "fake" medicine. In this broader sense, the placebo effect is a significant feature of medical practice and the supposed benefits of a placebo treatment appears to depend on the qualities of the patient–physician relationship.

Placebo agents are now commonly used in controlled clinical trials; research subjects are informed that they will be randomized and may receive either an active drug or an inert substance. There is no deception involved and this practice is certainly ethical. Placebo administration appears to have become rare in clinical medicine, although it may be occasionally considered.

The problem of deception arises when the physician knows that the intervention does not have the objective properties necessary for efficacy and when the patient is kept ignorant of this fact. Examples: weekly shots of vitamin B for fatigue but without a diagnosis of pernicious anemia; penicillin administered for a nonbacterial infection. In some cases, the deception is an outright moral offense, motivated solely by the desire to keep the patient's fees or to "get the patient off my back." In other cases placebo deception may raise a genuine ethical question. The duty not to deceive seems to conflict with the duty to benefit without doing harm.

CASE I. A 73-year-old widow lives with her son. He brings her to a physician because she has become extremely lethargic and often confused. The physician determines that, after being widowed 2 years before, she had difficulty sleeping and had been prescribed hypnotics and that she is now addicted. The physician determines the best course would be to withdraw her from her present medication by a trial on placebos.

CASE II. A 62-year-old man has had a total proctocolectomy and ileostomy for colonic cancer. There is no evidence of remaining tumor; the wound is healing well and the ileostomy is functioning. On the eighth day after surgery, he complains of a crampy abdominal pain and requests medication. The physician first prescribes antispasmodic drugs, but the patient's complaints persist. The patient requests morphine, which had relieved his postoperative pain. The physician is reluctant to prescribe opiates. She believes the pain is psychological and knows that opiates will cause constipation. She contemplates a trial of placebo.

COMMENT. Any situation in which placebo use involves deliberate deception should be viewed as ethically perilous. The strong moral obligations of truthfulness and honesty prohibit deception; the danger to the patient–physician relationship (which is the most important nondeceptive placebo) advises against it. In those situations, however, when deceptive placebo use seems indicated, its ethical use rests on the following conditions: (1) the condition to be treated should be known as one that has high response rates to placebo, for example, mild mental depression or postoperative pain; (2) the alternative to placebo is either continued illness or the use of a drug with known toxicity, for example, monoamine oxidase inhibitors or morphine; (3) the patient wishes to be treated and cured, if possible; (4) the patient insists on a prescription.

COUNSEL. When the above conditions are present, it is ethical to use a "deceptive" placebo. This is justified because, in an important sense, the placebo is known to be an effective agent, is harmless (although there can be placebo toxicity), and is an alternative to a more harmful drug. Thus, we consider the use of a placebo in Case I is not justified. The patient is not demanding. The problem of addiction should be confronted directly. There will be ample opportunity to develop a good relationship with this patient. Subsequent discovery of deception might undermine this relationship. Use of placebo in Case II may be ethically permissible. The patient is demanding relief. Morphine is dangerous. A short trial of placebo may be effective in relieving pain and avoiding harm. Also, the cause of this late postoperative pain may be masked by use of opiates. Still, patient explanation may be as effective and less perilous to the therapeutic relationship than placebo use. The deceptive placebo can destroy the trust that creates the important and therapeutic "placebo effect."

2.5 REFUSAL OF TREATMENT BY PERSONS WITH CAPACITY TO CHOOSE

Persons who are apparently informed and are not incapacitated sometimes refuse recommended treatment. When the treatment is elective, ethical problems are unlikely. However, if care is judged necessary to save life or manage serious disease, physicians may be confronted with an ethical problem: Does the physician's responsibility to help the patient ever override the patient's freedom? This problem is sometimes called the problem of paternalism, overriding the preferences of a person in order to benefit that person or to prevent him/her from being harmed. (EB: RIGHT TO REFUSE MEDICAL TREATMENT).

2.5.1 **Competent Refusal.**   Refusal of care by a competent and informed adult should be respected, even if that refusal leads to serious harm to the individual. In Case [2.2.5], Mr. K. M. refuses hospitalization after suspected MI. The physician should record the fact and circumstances of the patient's refusal. [See Bartling 3.2.7.]

2.5.2 **Refusal on Grounds of Unusual Belief**

CASE.   Mr. G. comes to a physican for treatment of peptic ulcer. He says he is a Jehovah's Witness. He is a firm believer and knows his disease is one that may eventually require administration of blood. He quotes the Biblical passage on which he bases his belief: "That ye abstain from meats offered to idols and from blood . . ." (Acts 15:28). The physician inquires of her Episcopal clergyman about the interpretation of this passage. He reports, after some research, that no Christian denomination except the Jehovah's Witnesses takes it to prohibit transfusion. The physician considers Mr. G.'s belief both unreasonable in view of his health needs and unfounded in religious tradition. She also considers his preferences impose an inferior standard of care. What sort of "contract" should the physician make with this patient? (EB: BLOOD TRANSFUSION.) [See 2.1–2.1.4; 2.2.8.]

COMMENT. (a) As a general principle, the unusual beliefs and choices of other persons should be tolerated if they pose no threat to other parties. The ethical principle of autonomy requires that these beliefs and choices be respected, even though they appear mistaken to others. If, however, unusual beliefs do pose a threat to others it is ethically permissible and even obligatory to prevent harm by means commensurate with the imminence of the threat and the seriousness of the harm. Courts have, in recent years, upheld the legal right of adult Jehovah's Witnesses to refuse lifesaving transfusions. Courts have, however, intervened to order blood transfusions for the children of Jehovah's Witnesses. [5.2.5–5.2.6].

(b) Refusal of blood transfusion differs in a significant way from a refusal of all therapy or of recommended treatments (e.g., the cases in 2.2.5 of the young man with meningitis and the man with MI. The Jehovah's Witnesses acknowledge the reality of their illness and desire to be cured or cared for; they simply reject one modality of care. Physicians may feel this limitation involves them in substandard and incompetent medical care. This is the essence of the ethical problem posed by the Jehovah's Witness.

(c) The physician's inquiry about the interpretation of the biblical passage is interesting. Presumably, she would feel more comfortable with a belief she knew to be part of her own religious tradition. Also, it might show an inclination to consider "conscientious beliefs" as those that are instilled in persons by God or religious authority (as the American courts long did with conscientious objectors to war). It is our opinion that the validity of a belief in terms of an orthodox tradition is not relevant. Rather, the sincerity of those who hold it and their ability to understand its consequences for their lives is the relevant issue in this sort of case.

COUNSEL. (a) Jehovah's Witnesses cannot be considered incapacitated to make choices unless there is clinical evidence of such incapacity. This evidence should be developed as rigorously as for any other case of suspected incapacity. Anecdotes suggest physicians may be inclined to sweep the Jehovah's Witnesses into the category of the incapacitated because of their unusual belief. On the contrary, these persons are usually quite clear about their belief and its consequences. It is a prominent part of their faith, insistently taught and discussed. Witnesses have a long history of standing by this belief. Thus, while others may consider it irrational, adherence is not, in itself, a sign of incapacity.

(b) If the Jehovah's Witness comes as a medical patient, the eventual possibility of the use of blood should be discussed and a clear agreement worked out between physician and patient about treatment in that eventuality. It should be learned whether the patient rejects autotransfusion and dialysis as well as blood and blood products. The availability of blood substitutes should be discussed; under no circumstances should the physician resort to deception. A physician who, in conscience, cannot accept being held to an inferior or dangerous standard of care should withdraw from the case.

(c) If the Jehovah's Witness is in need of emergency care and refuses blood transfusion, the refusal should be considered decisive unless there is some clinical evidence of incapacity to make a responsible decision. Should the patient, who is known to be a confirmed believer, be incapacitated, it can be presumed that the refusal represents the person's true wishes. If little is known about the patient and his or her status as a believer cannot be authenticated, treatment should be provided. In the face of uncertainty about personal preferences, it is our position that response to the patient's medical need should take ethical priority.

2.5.3　**Enigmatic Refusal.**　On occasion, refusal of care may appear enigmatic: it is difficult to discern why a person should refuse an obvious benefit or even difficult to discern whether they are really refusing.

> CASE.　In the ACURE case [1.3] a young man presented with signs and symptoms suggestive of bacterial meningitis. When he was told his diagnosis and told he would be admitted to the hospital for treatment with antibiotics, he refused, without giving a reason. The physician explained the extreme dangers of going untreated and the minimal risk of treatment. The young man persisted in his refusal. Other than this strange adamancy, he exhibited no evidence of mental derangement or altered mental status. [See 2.2.2–2.2.4.]

COMMENT.　In this case the initial consent for diagnosis was implicit in the young man's presenting himself at the clinic. However, the patient's enigmatic refusal introduced an incongruence between medical indications and patient preference. It might be argued that the physician should simply permit the patient to refuse treatment since the patient showed no objective signs of incapacitation or serious psychiatric impairment. However, in ACURE where the risk of treatment is low and the benefit is great and the risk of nontreatment is high and the "benefits" of nontreatment are small, it is ethically obligatory for the physician to probe further to determine why the patient desires to refuse treatment. Despite the explanation given, has the patient somehow failed to understand and appreciate the nature of the condtion or the benefits and risks of treatment and nontreatment? If patients understand the explanation, are they denying that they are ill? Or is the patient acting on the basis of some unexpressed fear, mistaken belief, or irrational desire? Through further discussion with the patient some of these questions might be answered. Assume, however, there is no evidence that the patient fails to understand and nothing emerges to indicate denial, fear, mistake, or irrational belief. Some might then ask, should the patient's enigmatic refusal be respected? Since the medical condition is so serious, should treatment proceed even against the patient's will? This case poses a genuine ethical conflict between the patient's personal autonomy and the paternalistic values that favor medical intervention. A clinical decision must be made quickly to treat or release the patient; good ethical reasons can be given for either alternative.

COUNSEL. This patient's refusal is truly enigmatic. There is no evidence of incapacity to choose due to altered mental state (although the patient's high fever might lead the physician to suspect some derangement). Further, there is no expression of an "unusual belief," for example, a religious objection to antibiotics. The patient simply refuses and will provide no reason for the refusal. Given both this enigmatic refusal and the urgent, serious need for treatment, we counsel the patient be treated, even against his will, if this is possible. Should there be time, legal authorization should be sought. In offering this counsel, we have come down, with some reluctance, in favor of paternalistic intervention at the expense of personal autonomy. Our reluctance stems from the unwillingness to violate the liberty of another. It is overcome by the consideration that something essential is missing in this case. It is difficult to believe this young man wishes to die. The conscientious physician faces two evils: to honor a refusal that might not represent the patient's true preferences, thus leading to the patient's death, or to override the refusal in the hope that, subsequently, the patient will recognize the benefit. This is a genuine moral dilemma: The principle of beneficence and the principle of autonomy seem to dictate contradictory courses of action. In medical care, dilemmas cannot merely be contemplated; they must be resolved. Thus, we resolve it in favor of treatment against the wishes of this patient.

FURTHER COMMENT. In this case, we accept as ethically permissible the unauthorized treatment of an apparently competent person. In Case I [2.2.5], we allowed Mr. K. M., a man with the MI, to leave the hospital. We would consider attempts to restrain him ethically impermissible. What considerations lead us to these apparently inconsistent conclusions?

(a) The medical indications are significantly different. Mr. ACURE has a critical disease, and low-risk treatment will be effective in preventing serious harm. There is an opportunity for complete achievement of all medical goals. The patient with the MI resembles ACURE cases in many respects: The patient suffers from an acute, critical problem. However, unlike Mr. ACURE's problem, this critical episode is not directly treatable nor reversible. Observation is advisable in order to be able to intervene in case of life-threatening arrhythmias or heart failure. However, observation, requiring admission, may itself be risky since it may increase the anxiety of an already anxious man resisting hospitalization.

(b) The consent situation is significantly different. In neither case is there behavioral evidence of psychiatric impairment, yet in both, the common psychological mechanism of denial hinders good judgment. However, in the case of Mr. K. M., the refusal takes place after a full disclosure of the problem and its risks. There has been opportunity to discuss, persuade and argue. He responds that he feels better and wants to go home. He has business that cannot be delayed. In Mr. ACURE's case, discussion is truncated. Efforts to discuss are rejected. Yet he has willingly come to be treated. There is a strong suspicion that some crucial element of this negotiation is missing. It is that suspicion which leads the physicians, given the medical situation, to treat him against his wishes.

(c) In fact, something *was* missing. Mr. ACURE's cousin had died several years ago of an anaphylactic reaction to penicillin. Mention of antibiotics had triggered a psychological response of denial, which manifested itself in a refusal without reason. (Indeed, the patient had no recall of these events when recovered.) The circumstances of his particular illness drew the physicians in the direction of rapid, perhaps careless and hasty, treatment. They did not have the time or the inclination to understand the patient's inarticulate refusal of penicillin.

(d) The case illustrates that physicians are often pressured by circumstances to make decisions before all relevant information is known. Thus, the rightness or wrongness of the clinical decision always must be assessed in terms of what the clinician knew or should have known at the time of the decision. In this case the physician *should* have known more. There is a tendency in medicine—in evaluating the rightness of both clinical and ethical decisions—to base such assessments on data that become available long after the decision had to be made. We include this complex and troubling case to illustrate how actual situations do, at times, yields ambiguous results. One can only strive to make decisions that are as fully and as carefully analyzed as the circumstances permit.

.5.4 **Refusal of Information.**   Persons have a right to information about themselves. Similarly, they have the right to refuse information or to ask the physician not to inform them. Some patients may prefer to trust the doctor to make the proper decisions. If this is clearly the patient's preference, it should be respected. On occasion, it will cause an ethical problem.

> CASE.   In the CARE case [1.4] the patient with MS had shown little interest during the early years of his illness in learning about the possible course of his disease. He even refused several offers by the physician to discuss this. However, on one of his repeated admissions for treatment of urinary tract infections, he states that, had he known what his life would be like, he would have refused permission for treatment of other life-

threatening acute problems. The patient's mental status is difficult to evaluate; some think he shows signs of early dementia.
Should be have been informed of his prognosis at an earlier
time even though unwilling to engage in such discussions with
his physician?

COMMENT.   In this case we are concerned with what the physician communicates and should communicate about diagnosis
and, particularly, prognosis. Should the physician override the
patient's stated preference not to know about his condition?
Should physicians withhold unpleasant information about prognosis to protect the patient from depression or other negative, potentially damaging emotions? Or should the patient be told, as
soon as a reliable diagnosis has been made, enough to maximize
his opportunity to plan his life in the face of future prospects? Although it is tempting to withhold information to protect the patient, a better alternative would be to give the patient general information sufficient to indicate the seriousness of his condition as
well as the uncertainty about the time, the severity, and the extent
of the problems that MS can cause. The middle ground avoids the
extremes of withholding too much too long or disclosing too
much too soon. Considerable discretion is required to find the
proper balance of disclosure and tact. Furthermore, the disclosures made as the condition worsens must be adjusted in the light
of the impairments to the patient's competence. In some cases of
late-stage MS an associated dementia appears. Thus it would be
advisable to make disclosures before the patient's capacity is so
severely impaired that he cannot understand.

COUNSEL.   Again we have a difficult case in which unpleasant
but unavoidable moral choices must be made. Here we opt for
more rather than less disclosure, especially because the condition,
though untreatable, is long-lasting. Thus the patient's long-term
moral autonomy is respected more by providing as much information as possible to enable him to make more choices while he is
physically and mentally able to learn coping mechanisms in advance. The short-term gains of ignorance are outweighed by the
long-term benefits of knowledge.

2.5.5   **Paternalism.**   The cases in 2.5 all pose the problem of paternalism. Paternalistic behavior, that is, overriding a person's ex-

pressed preferences for the person's own benefit is, in general, ethically reprehensible. However, such behavior is justifiable when all these conditions seem present: (1) the person appears to have some defect or incumbrance in understanding or deciding, (2) serious harm is likely unless there is intervention, (3) the probable benefit from intervention will outweigh the probable harm of nonintervention. Always, sound evidence of (1) is required; honest assessment of (2) and (3) are necessary. Finally, an attempt to acknowledge the patient's own values, insofar as they are known, should inform the evaluation of benefits and harms.

2.6   **THE LIVING WILL**

In recent years the document known as the living will has come into use. Many individuals prepare these documents in advance of the onset of serious illness as directions to their physicians concerning their medical treatment when they are dying. These documents typically contain such statements as "In case of serious illness from which I am unlikely to recover, I do not wish to be kept alive by heroic or extraordinary measures. I fear death less than the indignity of dependence and deterioration." The living will is a person's attempt to extend the expression of his or her preferences into a future when the actual expression will be impossible or difficult.

Even though the living will is not a legally binding instrument in the same way as a testamentary will, the spirit and intent of the writer should be taken seriously.

Some states have created legally sanctioned procedures allowing persons to exercise their right of choice after loss of competence. Natural Death Acts empower a person to refuse life-sustaining treatment in anticipation of incapacity. Durable Powers of Attorney authorize a competent person to appoint another to act as their proxy after loss of competence. Provisions for these differ from state to state. Even where a document of this sort has some legal authority, the physician to whom it is directed must interpret its meaning and application in the light of the patient's condition.

CASE I. A 70-year-old woman with severe hypertension suffers a stroke resulting in extensive paralysis. Her sister brings to the hospital a signed and witnessed living will, dated 1 year earlier. It contains the words," I fear death less than the indignity of dependence and deterioration.'' The patient is currently unable to communicate. She is intubated and has cardiac arrhythmias. Should the physician, on become aware of her living will, extubate her? Should no-code orders be written in anticipation of cardiac arrest? [See 1.4–1.4.4.]

CASE II.   Mr. CARE, the patient with MS, is now hospitalized. He has suffered several respiratory arrests due to aspiration. His mental status is poor. He shows signs of organic brain syndrome. A question is raised about surgical placement of a tracheostomy tube. The patient's wife shows the physician a newspaper clipping describing the living will, with the note attached, ''I am dictating to my wife my approval of this living will. I want it to apply to me when necessary.'' Is this sufficient to direct the physician not to take measures to prevent another respiratory arrest?

COMMENT.   In both cases, evidence of personal preferences is being offered. In the first case there can be no doubt about the authenticity of the document, although its interpretation in the situation is difficult. The eventual effects of the stroke cannot be clearly predicted at this time; the extent to which the patient will experience ''the indignity of dependence and deterioration'' is unknown. Thus respect for her wishes is best manifested by continuing indicated medical treatment until her prognosis can be determined more clearly. In the second case there may be some question about the authenticity of the evidence, although the application is much clearer. The patient suffers from a lethal disease and is now in its terminal stages. Prevention of death by intermediate measures would only prolong an inevitable dying process. The expression of the patient's preferences, even though some doubt of its authenticity may exist, is helpful evidence for the clinician in considering whether to refrain from further intervention.

COUNSEL.   (a) When presented with a living will by a patient, discuss its meaning and implications fully with the patient. Learn what the patient means by vague expression such as ''heroic and extraordinary measures'' or ''dependence and deterioration.'' In the first case the patient, who did recover with very little residual deficit, stated that she meant ''she did not want to be a vegetable stuck with a lot of tubes.''

(b) If discussion with the patient is not possible, make reasonable efforts to determine the authenticity of the document: For example, ask relatives about the circumstances of its composition and about other expressions of preferences by the patient in conversations, letters, and the like. Examine the interests of other parties in the case of the patient. [See 4.2.] Interpret the meaning of the stated preferences in light of the medical indications for treatment [1.1.3] and the prognosis for future quality of life. [See 3.1–3.1.4.]

(c) Be aware of the exact legal meaning of such documents in the state in which you are practicing.

2.6.1 **Extraordinary and Ordinary Measures.** The terms "extraordinary" and "ordinary" appear in documents such as the living will. They are also frequently used in discussions about withholding or withdrawing life-supporting medical interventions. Often, the term "extraordinary" is used interchangeably with such terms as "heroic" or "unusual" measures. These usages are confusing and usually not very helpful in determining what should be done. However, Roman Catholic medical ethics, where the "ordinary-extraordinary" distinction originated, attempts to give these terms a more precise meaning. In this system the terms "ordinary" and "extraordinary" *do not* refer to the state of medical art (e.g., in 1925 blood transfusion was "extraordinary"; in 1960 chronic hemodialysis was "extraordinary"; today both are "ordinary"). Rather, the "extraordinary" nature of any treatment, regardless of how common and accepted as medical practice, refers to its impact on the personal, social, and even economic life of the patient and the patient's family. Roman Catholic moralists propose that persons had a moral obligation to preserve their lives and care for their health, but that this moral obligation demands only the use of "ordinary" means:

> Extraordinary means of preserving life are all medicines, treatments, and operations, which cannot be obtained or used without excessive expense, pain or other inconvenience for the patient or for others, or which, if used, would not offer a reasonable hope of benefit to the patient. [Kelley, G. *Medico Moral Problems*, St. Louis: Catholic Hospital Association, 1958, p. 135.]

It was left to the patient, with the advice of doctors, to determine what treatments were "extraordinary" in this sense. This interpretation of ordinary–extraordinary was endorsed by the President's Commission on the Study of Ethical Problems in Medicine and Biomedical and Behavioral Research, which suggested the words "proportionate–disproportionate" be substituted to indicate more clearly the relationship between the burdens and benefits coming to the patient or to others [President's Commission. *Deciding to Forego Life-sustaining Treatment*, Chapter 2; see General References]. In this sense, the form of treatment, its complexity or its invasiveness is not the relevant factor: only the burden it imposes in relations to the benefit it brings.

2.7   **SURROGATE DECISIONS**

When a patient is thought to be incapacitated to refuse treatment—or even to consent to treatment—it is a common mistake to suppose a family member may consent on behalf of the patient. In most states the law *does not* permit family members—unless they have been legally authorized by court order granting guardianship to do so—to consent to or refuse medical care on behalf of an adult family member, incapacitated or not. Physicians must be familiar with the law of the jurisdiction. In addition, mere suspicion of incapacity does not give physicians the authority to treat the patient against the patient's wishes unless a determination of incompetence has been legally obtained according to local laws and regulations, and an authorization to treat has been granted by court order or by the consent of the patient's guardian or conservator. [See 1.3–1.3.3, 2.2, 4.2, 5.2.]

2.7.1 **Surrogate Decision-Makers.** When someone other than a patient is granted authority to decide in behalf of the patient, their decisions must promote the patient's welfare. This is determined in two ways:

(a) if the patient has been able to express preferences in the past and has done so, the surrogate must use knowledge of these preferences in making the decision ("substituted judgment").

(b) if the patient's own preferences are unknown or unclear, the proxy must consider the "best interests" of the patient, using some more objective, socially shared values, such as relief of suffering, preservation or restoration of function, extent and quality of life sustained. [See 3.1–3.3; 4.2.4; 5.3.2.]

2.7.2 **Implied Consent.** In some life-threatening emergency situations, patients are unable to express their preferences or to give their consent because they are unconscious or in shock. Physicians undertake lifesaving treatment without the express consent of the patient. This practice is legally justified as "implied consent": The patient can be presumed to want treatment and would give consent if able to do so. Implied consent is a legal fiction, inferred by the law from circumstances. It provides the physician with a defense against a subsequent charge of battery (although it may not defend against charges of negligence if the emergency treatment falls below acceptable standards of care). The principle of beneficence, which prescribes that a person in serious need must be helped by one who can do so (without harm or great inconvenience to the helper), is the ethical justification for treatment in life-threatening emergencies.

2.7.3 **Statutory Authority to Treat.** In all jurisdictions, statutes exist that authorize the physician to hold a person for treatment against the will of that person. These statutes pertain to persons who are suspected of suffering from mental disease, and the treatment authorized is treatment for mental disease. In addition, the person must be considered a danger to self or others. In some situations both mental disease and medical problems may be present.

> EXAMPLE. A 30-year-old man, known to the ER staff as psychotic and alcoholic, is brought to the hospital by a friend. He has been drinking and taking heroin and is hallucinating that Viet Cong are attacking him. He is breathless, has fainted twice in the last hour, and is incontinent of urine. He says his heart is breaking through his chest. Still, he says he has got to leave the hospital because it is being bombed. The admitting resident writes in the chart, "I noted hallucinations and psychotic ideation, thus, I am putting the patient on a medical hold and keeping him in the hospital for observation. Diagnosis: paroxysmal supraventricular tachycardia. Medications: haloperidol, digitalis. Further evaluation: assess electrolytes." [See 1.3–1.3.3.]

COMMENT. The question is whether the statutory "medical hold" allows medical treatment as well as treatment for mental illness. Each state's statute and local interpretations must be consulted for an answer. In general, the statutes seem to refer to mental illness alone as the justification for involuntary commitment and to its treatment as the sole permitted intervention. The question is probably not legally important if the treatment is lifesaving. In that case the legal doctrine of implied consent would suffice. If not lifesaving, but urgent and highly advisable, the physician is in a somewhat unclear situation. A clinical assessment of incapacity is made, but the patient has the legal right to refuse care unless declared incompetent. The use of the "medical hold" for medical as well as psychiatric treatment may be technically illegal, but it appears to make ethical sense.

2.7.4 **Consent of Minors.**   Person who are younger than the statutory age of consent (age 18 in all states) may seek the care of a physician. If their medical problem is not an emergency, such persons can be treated only with the consent of their parents. [See 5.2.] However, there are several exceptions.

(a) Almost all jurisdictions now have special provisions for the treatment of certain conditions without the consent of the minor's parents. These conditions are usually drug abuse and venereal disease (contraception, abortion, and mental illness are sometimes included, sometimes specifically excluded). Physicians should be aware of the provisions of the law in the jurisdiction in which they practice.

(b) The emancipated minor is a young person who lives independently of parents, physically, financially or otherwise. Married minors, those in the armed forces or living away at college are considered emancipated. They may request treatment and be treated without parental consent.

(c) The legal concept of "mature minor" is being increasingly invoked. A mature minor is one who is below statutory age and who is still dependent upon parents but who appears able to make reasoned judgments. These young persons pose something of a quandry to the physician from whom they seek care. On the one hand, they appear able to decide from themselves; on the other, their parents remain legally responsible for them. Legal authorities conclude the physician may respond to their requests under the following conditions:

(i) The patient is at the age of discretion (15 years or older) and appears able to understand the procedure and its risks sufficiently to be able to give a genuinely informed consent.

(ii) The medical measures are taken for the patient's own benefit (i.e., not as a transplant donor or research subject).

(iii) The measures can be justified as necessary by conservative medical opinion.

(iv) There is some good reason, including simple refusal by the minor to request it, why parental consent cannot be obtained.

COUNSEL.   A physician may treat a minor without parental consent if the minor is emancipated or if there is statutory authorization for certain sorts of treatment. If the minor does not fit either category but is capable of understanding and consent, the physician may treat under the conditions mentioned above.

In the case of the mature minor, however, the physician should inquire, if possible, about the reasons for the young person's unwillingness to communicate with parents. Steps should be taken, if the minor is willing, to attempt reconciliation or to solve the problem in a mutually satisfactory manner. Confidentiality should be maintained.

Physicians who honor the requests of mature minors are at some theoretical legal peril. However, "no decisions can be found within the past 20 years in which a parent recovered damages, even in the absence of a minor treatment statute, for treatment of a child over the age of 15 without parental consent" (Holder, 1977, p. 145).

A request for irreversible sterilization from a mature minor should probably never be honored. The legal reasons for this are the peril of suit by parents and by the minor at a later date. There are also statutory and regulatory prohibitions against sterilization of minors in certain federal programs and in many states. The ethical reason for refusal rests on the presumption that even a mature minor cannot comprehend the implications of this procedure as well as the likelihood of doing great harm.

2.8   **FAILURE TO COMPLY WITH MEDICAL REGIMEN**
The patient–physician relationship can be disrupted when patients who seek or need care fail to follow recommendations. This

lack of accord between physician preferences and patient preferences is commonly called noncompliance.

CASE. The COPE case (1.8) described a woman with diabetes
mellitus diagnosed 17 years ago. For the first 7 years after the
diagnosis she had frequent episodes of ketoacidiosis and hypoglycemia, even though she followed her dietary and medical
regimen. For the next 10 years her diabetes was well controlled.
Now consider the following developments in that case. After a
stormy divorce, the patient has changed in several ways. In the
3 years following divorce, she has gained 60 pounds and often
has not taken her insulin medication. She also has been drinking alcohol excessively and is often drunk. During these years,
she has required frequent admissions to the hospital for diabetic complications including: (1) ketoacidosis, (2) nonketotic
hyperosmolar state, (3) traumatic and poorly healing foot ulcers, and (4) alcohol-related problems. While in the hospital,
her diabetes is easier to manage, but even while in the hospital
she is frequently found in the cafeteria eating excessively. On
several occasions she has abused alcohol while in the hospital,
and at those times blood alcohol levels in excess of 200 mg %
were detected. Soon after discharge from the hospital, her diabetic control lapses.

Her physician is frustrated by her case. He blames the recurring
medical problems on the patient's unwillingness to participate
actively in her own care. The physician tells her she could easily
control her diabetic problem by merely resuming health habits
she had pursued 3 years previously, that is, by losing weight, by
taking her insulin regularly, and by drinking alcohol in modera-
tion. The patient is not averse to changing her life-style but on
discharge from the hospital she continues her poor health
habits. The physician urges her to have a psychiatric consultation. She agrees. The psychiatrist suggests a behavior modification program, which proves unsuccessful in changing her behavior. Finally, aversion therapy is suggested. Her physician
hesitates to advise her to participate in this program.

She continues to require hospitalization lasting 7 to 10 days
every month or two. After 10 years of working closely with this
patient, the physician considers withdrawing from the therapeutic relationship because he senses he is no longer able to help

the patient. The patient resists this suggestion. She complains the physician is merely trying to punish her for her alcoholism.

COMMENT. Patients such as Mrs. COPE are very frustrating to those who attempt to care for them. Occasionally the physician will accuse the patient (in words or in attitude) of being irresponsible. The patient engages constantly and apparently willfully in behavior that poses serious risk to health and even to life. Such patients place great strain on the doctor–patient relationship; often the accommodation between doctor and patient founders because of the strain.

Mrs. COPE's doctor contemplated withdrawing from her case. He judged she was simply irresponsible and that her behavior undermined the care he was attempting to provide. "Why keep this up?" he said. "It's useless. Whatever I do, she undoes." Is persistent irresponsibility relevant to an ethical decision to withdraw from a case? Can it ever be decisive?

NOTE. The accusation of irresponsibility can be an example of the ethical fallacy of "blaming the victim"; the actual fault may lie with a more powerful party who finds a way to lay the blame for his own failure on the ones who suffer its effects. The poor, for example, were accused of lack of ambition by industrialists who paid paltry wages for onerous work. Similarly, the apparent irresponsibility of patients may be an impression created by the failure of a physician to educate, support, and convey personal concern and interest in the patient. It may be more than an impression: Persons may be rendered incapable of caring responsibly for themselves by the way their physician deals with them. An excessive paternalism may stifle responsibility, while a lack of personal concern may encourage noncompliance.

COUNSEL. This patient's failure to comply with her medical regimen compromised her medical care. What, then, is the physician's responsibility?

(a) It is important to decide whether the patient is acting voluntarily or involuntarily. Most noncompliant behavior is voluntary in the sense that the patient demonstrates no signs of pathologic behavior. They either choose to ignore the regimen in favor of other behaviors they value more than health (a goal that, in an asymptomatic disease, may not seem very urgent or immediate) or fail in compliance because of such factors as irregular routine, complicated regimen, habitual forgetfulness, or poor explanation by the physician. Some noncompliance arises from profound emotional disturbance and ambivalence.

(b) If the physician judges that noncompliance arises from the patient's voluntary persistence in health risks, reasonable efforts at rational persuasion should be undertaken. If these fail, it is ethically permissible for the physician to adjust therapeutic goals and do the best in the circumstance; it is also ethically permissible to withdraw from the case, after advising the patient how to obtain care from other sources [See 2.9.1–2.10.]

(c) If external circumstances are the source of noncompliance, help should be provided to improve these circumstances. Many helpful stratagems have been suggested to correct obstacles of this sort.

(d) If noncompliance arises from psychological pathology, the physician has a strong ethical obligation to remain with the patient, adjusting treatment plans to the undesirable situation. Professional assistance in treating the pathology should be sought. The physician will experience great frustration, but the frustration is not, in itself, sufficient to justify leaving the patient. Additional circumstances, however, may contribute to a justification. [See 2.8.1, 2.8.2.]

(e) On rare occasions physicians may decide that no further treatment is indicated precisely because the patient's persistent behavior is so contrary to the goals of treatment. [See 2.8.2.]

2.8.1   **The Problem Patient: Noncritical.**   Noncompliance occurs in situations where the results, while harmful to the health of the patient, are not critical.

> CASE.   The patient presented in 2.8 is admitted for inpatient treatment of her obesity with a protein-sparing modified fasting regimen. She was found repeatedly in the cafeteria cheating on her diet. Her physician made reasonable efforts to persuade her to change her behavior.

COUNSEL. It would be ethically permissible for the physician to abandon therapeutic goals and to discharge the patient from the hospital. These goals were unachievable because of the patient's failure to participate in the treatment program.

2.8.2 **The Problem Patient: Critically Ill.** Is it ever justifiable to discharge a "problem" patient who has a critical illness requiring in-hospital treatment? Just as we believe that noncritically ill patients can be discharged if they repeatedly frustrate physicians' efforts to provide needed medical assistance, we also believe that noncooperation that directly counters the physician's effort can justify discharging a patient who is critically ill and in need of care. The situation, however, is more serious and requires added considerations before a decisive conclusion can be reached.

> CASE. R. A., a chronic intravenous drug abuser, is admitted for the third time in 3 years with a diagnosis of infective endocarditis. Three years before, he required mitral valve replacement for pseudomonas endocarditis, and 1 year ago he required replacement of the prosthetic valve after he developed staph aureus endocarditis. He now presents again with staph aureus endocarditis of the prosthetic valve.

> After 1 week of antibiotic therapy, he continues to have positive blood cultures. He consents to open heart surgery to replace again the infected mitral valve. For 10 days postoperatively (four in the intensive care unit) he is cooperative and compliant with his management and antibiotic treatment. On this treatment he becomes afebrile, and blood cultures are negative.

> He then begins to behave badly. He leaves his room and stays away for hours, often missing his dose of antibiotics. On several occasions a urine screening test demonstrates the presence of opiates and quinine, suggesting that he is using illicit narcotics even while being treated for infective endocarditis. On two separate occasions he punches nurses who scold him for being away from his room without permission. On the 11th postoperative day he is discovered by hospital security guards in his bathroom selling injectable narcotics to another patient. His roommate in the hospital had observed these dealings for several days, but the patient had threatened to kill the roommate if

he told anyone about these transactions. When all of this information becomes known to the patient's physician, the patient is asked to leave the hospital immediately. Despite the fact that the patient's infective endocarditis has not been treated optimally, he was discharged from the hospital against his will.

COMMENT. Consideration leading to an ethical justification of this decision are:

(a) *Medical indication.* The patient's use of intravenous street drugs at the same time that his physicians were attempting to eradicate his infective endocarditis indicated that the likelihood of medical success in this case, both short-term and long-term, was not great. Physicians are not obligated to treat people who simultaneously persist in actions that run directly counter to the goals of such treatment.

(b) *Patient preferences.* The patient wanted to be treated and, at the same time, to carry on his abusive and illegal behavior. The physicians are obliged to determine that the patient is competent to make such choices and that he was not suffering from a metabolic encephalopathy. [See 2.2.3.] On the other hand, the physicians are not obliged to deal with the patient's long-standing sociopathic behavior pattern.

(c) *Interests of other patients.* This patient's physicians (who were hospital-based) had obligations both to this patient and to their other hosptalized patients. This patient's behavior of selling narcotics to other inpatients and of terrorizing his roommate compromised the care other patients of the same physician were receiving. This patient, then, posed a direct and serious threat to other identifiable persons. [See 4.5.4.]

(d) *Institutional needs.* The institution must provide appropriate care for all of its admitted patients. By his actions of striking nurses and of arguing with doctors and of terrorizing other patients, this patient was undermining the ability of the hospital to carry out its responsibilities to other patients. [See Chapter 4.]

2.8.3 **The Problem Patient: Socially Unacceptable.** Our reasoning in this case does not apply to most patients who present with critical illnesses, even for those illnesses for which the patient might be held responsible.

EXAMPLE.   A 35-year-old chronic alcoholic with a long criminal record had emergency portacaval shunt for variceal bleeding. He continues to drink alcohol. Two years later, he presents twice within three months with acute bleeding from esophageal varices.

COUNSEL.   This patient should be managed with aggressive medical and surgical means in an effort to control his hemorrhage and to reverse his blood loss. It takes more than past behavior to warrant physicians' withdrawing from the treatment of serious illness; indeed, the patient's past history should be ignored in most cases except insofar as it is medically relevant. Rather, refusal to treat a patient can be ethically justified in view of a person's behavior in the present circumstances when that behavior makes achievement of medical goals impossible [as in 2.8.2].

COMMENT.   The problem with this patient is twofold. First, there is the suspicion that he will appear again, in the near future, with the same problem. Second, his problem was caused by personal behavior that is socially unacceptable, as is his lifestyle. The first problem raises the issues in Chapter 4 about allocation of scarce resources [4.5]; when the patient does become a repeater, the considerations mentioned there are relevant to a decision about his treatment. The second problem is discussed at 3.2.5. It should be noted that some harmful personal habits are more socially unacceptable than others. Substance abuse is strongly disapproved, while smoking, overeating, fast driving, not wearing seat belts, or engaging in dangerous sports are tolerated or even praised. Many conditions requiring expensive medical treatment are caused by behaviors that are socially accepted. Thus, singling out socially disapproved behaviors as less deserving of treatment reflects social prejudices rather than logic.

2.8.4   **Signing Out Against Medical Advice.**   Mr. R. A., the patient described in 2.8.2, might leave the hospital before physicians judge his treatment adequate. When patients do discharge themselves in this manner, most hospitals request them to sign a statement confirming that they are leaving against medical advice (AMA). Of course, the patients cannot be forced to sign the statement; they have the right to leave at will. The document merely provides legal evidence of the fact of the patient's voluntary departure and warning by the physician of the risks of leaving. This warning, carried out as patiently and carefully as possible, is the ethical duty of the physician.

2.9   EDUCATION, PERSUASION, AND COERCION

The cases presented in 2.8–2.8.3 illustrate some issues of education, persuasion, and coercion that are applicable to ethical problems encountered in the COPE model. It is the obligation of the physician to educate patients about the best means for ameliorating their illness. It is the obligation of physicians to try to persuade patients to follow a course designed to achieve these goals. Physicians' expertise often enables them to know more about the disease and its probable outcome than a patient knows. However, coercion is ethically unacceptable (conceding the line between persuasion and coercion may at times be blurred). Physicians should not engage in deception to trick patients into compliance. In 2.8.2 the disruptive patient clearly is beyond persuasion. The coercive acts of threatening him with expulsion and then forcing him to leave the hospital are justified only by his own coercive acts against others. (EB: BEHAVIOR CONTROL, BEHAVIORAL THERAPIES, FREE WILL AND DETERMINISM.)

2.9.1 **Withdrawing from Case.**   At times, in COPE situations that are not working out well, the physician may serve the patient best by deciding to dissolve the physican–patient relationship and by helping the patient to find another physician. As we noted in 1.1.3, the physician's principal goal is to help patients in the care of their health. If, for whatever reasons, this proves impossible, the physician may best demonstrate clinical judgment by withdrawing from the case and by finding another physician who might be more successful with the patient in these particular circumstances.

2.10   ABANDONMENT

Physicians who terminate the relationship with a patient sometimes wonder whether they can be charged with "abandonment." A legal definition of abandonment is "the unilateral severance by the physician of the professional relationship between himself and a patient without reasonable notice, at a time when there is still the necessity of continued medical attention" [McIntyre, 1962].

Charges of abandonment can arise when the physician simply ceases to care for the patient without notice or when the physician is dilatory and careless (e.g., failure to visit the patient in the hospital or failing to judge the patient's condition serious enough to warrant attention). A charge of abandonment can usually be countered by showing that the patient did receive warning in sufficient time to arrange for medical care. There is no legal obligation on the physician to arrange for further care from another physician, although there is a legal obligation to provide full medical records to the new attending physician. If the physician does intend to maintain the relationship with the patient but will be unavailable for a time, there is a legal obligation to arrange for coverage by another physician. Failure to do so can be construed as abandonment.

Even though legal requirements have been met, a physician may be ethically blamed for abandoning a patient. If the patient is in need of care and has no other recourse, the physician has an ethical obligation to continue, despite provocation. That obligation is, of course, limited by several conditions. If the patient absorbs excessive time and energy, creating risk to other patients, if the patient is acting in ways to frustrate the attainable medical goals, or if the patient is endangering others by overt action, any ethical obligation to continue care would be diminished. These conditions appear to be verified in 2.8.2.

2.10.1   **Conscientious Objection by the Physician.**   Physicians have their own moral values. Patients may express preferences that the physician finds morally objectionable. Traditionally, medical ethics has required physicians to abstain from moral judgments about their patients in regard to medical care. *Examples*: An ER physician is expected to provide competent care to the wounded assailant of an elderly person as well as to the assaulted party; a physician should treat, without censure, venereal disease contracted in what the physician considers an immoral liaison.

On occasion physicians may be asked not merely to tolerate what they consider immorality but to participate in effecting an immoral action desired by the patient. *Examples*: A male patient requests a physician who considers transsexualism morally wrong to prescribe female estrogens in order to promote secondary female sexual characteristics; a Catholic physician is asked to perform an abortion.

Physicians may refuse to cooperate in actions they judge immoral on grounds of conscience. It is important, in forming one's conscience, to separate the moral values to which one is committed from personal distaste or prejudice. *Example*: A physician refuses to undertake care of a Jehovah's Witness with a hemorrhagic diathesis "on moral grounds," while in fact the physician does not like to feel impotent or run the risk of "losing a patient." Institutions and programs should establish policy about conscientious objection and make the policy clear to those who work in that institution or program. (EB: CIVIL DISOBEDIENCE IN HEALTH SERVICES.)

BIBLIOGRAPHY

2.0–2.1 *Autonomy*

Angell, M. Respecting the autonomy of competent patients. N Eng J Med, 1984, 310:1115.

Beauchamp, T.L., Childress, J.F. *Principles of Biomedical Ethics*, Chapter 3. (See General References.)

Brody, D.S. The patient's role in decision-making. Ann Intern Med, 1980, 93:718.

Burnham, S. Dialectic is diagnostic. Ann Intern Med, 1984, 100:899.

Cassell, E.J. *The Healer's Art: A New Approach to the Doctor-Patient Relationship.* Philadelphia: J.B. Lippincott, 1976.

Cassell, E.J. *Talking to Patients,* Cambridge, Mass.: MIT Press. 1983.

Childress, J., Siegler, M. Metaphors and models of doctor–patient relationship. Theor Med, 1984, 5:17.

Cousins, N. The physician as communicator. JAMA, 1982, 248:587.

Cousins, N. Anatomy of an illness (As perceived by the patient). N Engl J Med, 1976, 295:1458.

Eisenberg, J.M. Sociologic influences on decision making by clinicians. Ann Intern Med, 1979, 90:957.

Eraker, S., Politser, P. How decisions are reached: Physician and patient. Ann Intern Med, 1982, 97:262.

Fiore, N. Fighting cancer—one patient's perspective. N Engl J Med, 1979, 300:284.

Greenfield, S., Kaplan, S., Ware, J. Expanding patient involvement in care. Ann Intern Med, 1985, 102:520.

Martin, A.R. Exploring patient beliefs. Arch Intern Med, 1983, 143:1773.

Quill, T. Partnerships in patient care: A contractual approach. Ann Intern Med, 1983, 98:228.

Reiser, S.J. Words as scalpels: Transmitting evidence in the clinical dialogue. Ann Intern Med, 1980, 92:837.

Siegler, M. The Doctor–patient accommodation: A central event in clinical medicine. Ann Intern Med, 1982, 142:1899.

Siegler, M. Searching for moral certainty in medicine. Bull NY Acad Med 1981; 57:56.

Szaz, T.S., Hollender, M.H. The basic models of the doctor–patient relationship. Arch Intern Med, 1956, 97:585.

Vanderpool, H. Patient truthfulness: A test of ethical models of the physician patient relationship. J Med Phil, 1984, 9:353.

Waitzkin, H. Doctor—patient communication. JAMA, 1984, 252:2441.

Winslade, W., Ross, J. *Choosing Life or Death: A Guide for Patients, Families and Professionals*. New York: Free Press. 1986.

2.2 *Competence*

Cassel, C., Jameton, A. Dementia in the elderly: An analysis of moral responsibility. Ann Intern Med, 1981, 94:802.

Drane, J. Competency to give an informed consent. JAMA, 1984, 252:925.

Gert, B., Culver, C. *Philosophy in Medicine: Conceptual and Ethical Issues in Medicine and Psychiatry.* New York: Oxford University Press, 1982.

Golden, J., Johnston, G. Problems of distortion in doctor–patient relationships. Psychiatry Med, 1970, 1:127.

Kapp, M. Treatment of incompetent patients. JAMA, 1984, 251:2514.

McCullough, L. Medical care for elderly patients with diminished competence: An ethical analysis. J Am Geriat Soc, 1984, 32:150.

Meyers, D. *Medicolegal Implications*, Chapter 6. (See General References.)

Perl, M., Shelp, E. Psychiatric consultation masking moral dilemmas in medicine. N Engl J Med, 1982, 307:618.

President's Commission for the Study of Ethical Problems in Medicine and Biomedical and Behavioral Research. *Deciding to Forego Life-Sustaining Treatment* (see General References).

President's Commission for the Study of Ethical Problems in Medicine and Biomedical and Behavioral Research. *Making Health Care Decisions*. (See General References.)

Roth, L., Meisel, A., Lidz, C. Tests of competency to consent to treatment. Am J Psychiatry, 1977, 134:279.

Schneiderman, L., Arras, J. Counseling patients to counsel physicians on future care in the event of patient incompetence. Ann Intern Med, 1985, 102:693.

Winograd, C. Mental status tests and the capacity for self care. J Am Geriat Soc, 1984, 32:49.

2.3 *Informed Consent*

Barber, B. *Informed Consent in Medical Therapy and Research*. New Brunswick, N.J.: Rutgers University Press, 1980.

Cassileth, B., Zupkin, R., Sutton-Smith, K., March, V. Informed consent—why are its goals imperfectly realized? N Engl J Med, 1980, 302:896.

Cassileth, B., Zupkin, R., Sutton-Smith, K., March, V. Information and participation preferences among cancer patients. Ann Intern Med, 1980, 92:832.

Faden, A., Faden, R. Informed consent in medical practice with particular reference to neurology. Arch Neurol, 1978, 35:761.

Faden, R., Beauchamp, T. Informed consent and decision making: The impact of disclosed information. Social Indicators Res, 1980, 7:313.

Katz, J. *The Silent World of Physician and Patient*. New York: Free Press, 1985.

Lidz, C.W., Meisel, A., Osterweis, M., et al. Barriers to informed consent. Ann Intern Med, 1983, 99:539.

McNeil, B., et al. On the elicitation of preferences for alternative therapy. N Engl J Med, 1982, 302:1259.

Meisel, A., Roth, L. What we do and do not know about informed consent. JAMA, 1981, 246:2473.

Miller, L. Informed consent I–IV. JAMA, 1980, 244:2100, 2347, 2556, 2661.

President's Commission for the Study of Ethical Problems in Medicine and Biomedical and Behavioral Research. *Making Health Care Decisions*. (See General References.)

Rosoff, A. *Informed Consent: A Guide for Health Care Providers*. Rockville, Md. Aspen Systems, 1981.

Strull, W., Lo, B., Charles, G. Do patients want to participate in medical decision making? JAMA, 1984, 252:2990.

2.4 *Truth Telling*

Bok, S. The ethics of giving placebos. *Scientific American,* 1974, 231(5):17. [In Reiser, Dyke, Curran, (eds.); *Ethics in Medicine*, p. 248. See General References.]

Bok, S. *Lying. Moral Choice in Public and Private Life*. New York: Pantheon Books, 1978.

Brody, H. The lie that heals: The ethics of giving placebos. Ann Intern Med, 1982, 97:112.

Cabot, R.C. The use of truth and falsity in medicine. *American Med,* 1903, 5:344. [In Reiser, Dyke, Curran, (eds.), *Ethics in Medicine,* 1977; 213. See General References.]

Cousins, N. A layman looks at truthtelling in medicine. JAMA, 1980, 24:1929.

Goodwin, J., Goodwin, J., Vogel, A. Knowledge and use of placebos by nurses and house officers. Ann Intern Med, 1979, 91:111.

Novack, D., Plumer, R., Smith, R., et al. Changes in physician's attitudes toward telling the cancer patient. JAMA, 1979, 241:897.

Oken, D. What to tell cancer patients: A study of medical attitudes. JAMA, 1961, 175:1120.

Shapiro, A. Factors contributing to the placebo effect. Am J Psychother, 1964, 18(Suppl):73.

Shapiro, A. The placebo effect in the history of medical treatment. Am J Psychiatry, 1959, 116:298.

Sheldon, M. Truth telling in medicine. JAMA, 1982, 247:651.

Silber, T. Placebo therapy: The ethical dimension. JAMA, 1979, 242:245.

Simmons, B. Problems in deceptive medical procedures: An ethical and legal analysis of administration of placebos. J Med Ethics, 1978, 4:172.

2.5–2.7 *Refusal of Care/Decisions to Forego*

Applebaum, P., Roth, L. Patients who refuse treatment in medical hospitals. JAMA, 1983, 250:1296.

Buchanan, A. Medical paternalism. Philos Pub Affairs, 1977, 7:370.

Childress, J. *Who Should Decide? Paternalism in Health Care.* New York: Oxford University Press, 1983.

Dixon, J., Smalley, M. Jehovah's Witnesses: the surgical–ethical challenge. JAMA, 1981, 246:2471.

Eisendrath, S., Jonsen, A. The living will. JAMA, 1983, 249:2054.

Faden, R., Faden, A. False belief and the refusal of medical treatment. J Med Ethics, 1977, 3:133.

Gert, B., Culver, C. Paternalistic behavior. Philos Pub Affairs, 1976, 6:45.

Ford, J. Refusal of blood transfusions by Jehovah's Witnesses. Catholic Lawyer, 1964, 10:212.

Imbus, S., Zawacki, B. Autonomy for burned patients when survival is unprecedented. N Engl J Med, 1977, 297:308.

Jackson, D., Younger, S. Patient autonomy and 'death with dignity'. Some clinical caveats. N Engl J Med, 1979, 301:404.

Jonsen, A. Blood transfusion and Jehovah's Witnesses: The impact of the patient's unusual beliefs in critical care. Crit Care Clin, 1986.

Jonsen, A. Involuntary treatment in medicine. Annu Rev Med, 1986, 37:41.

Jonsen, A. Dying right in California: The California Natural Death Act. Clin Res, 1978, 26:55.

Kelly, G. *Medico-Moral Problems.* St. Louis: Catholic Hospital Association, 1958.

Lo, B., Jonsen, A. Ethical decisions in the care of a patient terminally ill with metastatic cancer. Ann Intern Med, 1980, 92:107.

McCartney, J. The development of the doctrine of ordinary and extraordinary means of preserving life in Catholic moral theology before the Karen Quinlan Case. Linacr Q, 1980, 47:215.

Macklin, R. Consent, coercion and conflict of rights. Perspect Biol Med, 1977, 20:360.

Meyers, D. *Medicolegal Implications,* Chapters 10 and 11. (See General References.)

O'Neil, R. In defense of the ordinary-extraordinary distinction. Linacr Q, 1978, 45:37.

Perry, C., Applegate, W. Medical paternalism and patient self-determination. J Am Geriat Soc, 1985, 33:353.

President's Commission for the Study of Ethical Problems in Medicine and Biomedical and Behavioral research. *Deciding To Forego Life-Sustaining Treatment.* (See General References.)

Siegler, M. Critical illness: The limits of autonomy. Hastings Cent Rep, 1977, 7(5):12.

Siegler, M., Goldblatt, A.D. Clinical intuition: A procedure for balancing the rights of patients and the responsibilities of physicians. In *The Law–Medicine Relation: A Philosophical Exploration.* S. Spicker, J.M. Healy, H.T. Englehardt (eds). Boston and Dordrecht: D. Reidel, 1981.

Steinbrook, R., Lo, B. Decision making for incompetent patients by designated proxy. N Engl J Med, 1984, 310:1598.

Suber, D.G., Tabor, W.J. Withholding of life sustaining treatment from the terminally ill incompetent patient: Who decides? JAMA, 1982, Part I, 248:2250; Part II, 248:2431.

Thomasma, D. Beyond paternalism and patient autonomy. Ann Intern Med, 1983, 98:243.

Veatch, R. Limits of guardian treatment refusal: A reasonableness standard. Am J Law Med, 1984, 9:427.

2.8–2.10 *Compliance and so forth*

Anderson, R. J., Kirk, L.M. Methods of improving patient compliance in chronic disease states. Arch Intern Med, 1982, 142:1673.

Curran, C.E. Cooperation: Toward a revision of the concept. Linacr Q, 1974, 41:152.

Curran, W. Breaking off the physician–patient relationship: Another legal hazard. N Engl J Med, 1982, 307:1058.

Eraker, S.A., Kirscht, J., Becker, M. Understanding and improving patient compliance. Ann Intern Med, 1984, 100:258.

Gaylin, W. On the borders of persuasion: A psychoanalytic look at coercion. Psychiatry, 1974, 37:1.

Groves, J. Taking care of the hateful patient. N Engl J Med, 1978, 298:883.

Jonsen, A. Ethical issues in compliance. In Compliance in Health Care. C. Haynes, D. Taylor, D. Sackett (eds). Baltimore: Johns Hopkins University Press, 1979.

McIntyre, L. The action of abandonment in medical malpractice litigation. Tulane Law Rev, 1962, 36:834.

Mahadon, H.J., Gerson, S., Ryback, R. Managing care of the difficult patient in the emergency unit. JAMA, 1984, 252:2585.

Veatch, R. Voluntary risks to health. JAMA, 1980, 243:50.

Wickler, D. Persuasion and coercion for health: Ethical issues in government efforts to change life styles. Health and society. Milbank Mem Q, 1978, 56:303.

Winterbottom, S. Coping with the violent patient in accident and emergency. J Med Ethics, 1979, 5:124.

3

QUALITY OF LIFE

3.0 This chapter concerns quality of life insofar as that subject influences clinical ethical decisions. It discusses (1) the meaning of this phrase in clinical ethical deliberations, (2) the use of quality-of-life judgments in decisions to terminate or withhold therapy, (3) the related concept of "quality of death" in discussions of euthanasia, (4) use of pain medication for dying persons; and (5) suicide.

The competent practice of medicine aspires to improve the quality of life of patients. The goals of medicine envision this improvement in quality of life: restoration of health, relief of pain and symptoms, and support of compromised function. There is little question about medicine's dedication to enhancing quality of life, but there are many questions about what quality of life consists of, about who determines quality of life, and about the effects of such judgments on the care provided to the patient.

The ethical principles underlying the considerations in this chapter are complex. Considerations of quality of life enter into decisions to act in accord with the principle of beneficence, that is, to do good and avoid harm. These considerations also arise in the utilitarian form of ethical deliberation, which involves, in part, the intention to effect a greater balance of pleasure over pain in the experiences of a person, of a population, or in the world. (EB: ETHICS, UTILITARIANISM.)

3.1   **MEANING OF QUALITY OF LIFE**

The phrase "quality of life" is frequently heard in clinical discussions about ethical problems. Frequent use has given the phrase neither any precise meaning nor any definite application. It seems an attempt to put a value upon some feature, or collection of features, of human experience. As such, it is highly subjective; yet the phrase is often used by someone other than the person who is living the life being evaluated. Also, the phrase is used as if there were certain objective criteria, even though, as an evaluation, it rests less on facts than upon preferences about those facts. (EB: LIFE, QUALITY OF LIFE, VALUE OF LIFE.)

3.1.1   **Definition.**   "Quality of life" is a phrase that does not lend itself to satisfactory definition. Still, common use seems to support two definitions relevant to clinical discussions:

(a) *The subjective satisfaction expressed or experienced by an individual in his or her physical, mental, and social situation* (even though these may be deficient in some manner).

> EXAMPLE I.   A 23-year-old gymnastics instructor who is paralyzed due to a spinal cord lesion may say, "My life isn't as bad as it looks: I've come to terms with my loss and discovered the powers of my mind."

> EXAMPLE II.   A 68-year-old artist who is a chronic diabetic now faces blindness and multiple amputations. She says: "I wonder if I can endure a life of such poor quality?"

(b) *The subjective evaluation by an onlooker of another's subjective experiences of personal life.*

> EXAMPLE I.   A parent says of a 29-year-old retarded son with an IQ of 40, "He used to be so easy, but he's become so difficult—what kind of quality of life does he have?"

EXAMPLE II.   An 83-year-old woman with advanced senile dementia, who is bedridden and tube-fed is described by the
nurses as "having poor quality of life."

COMMENT.   The invocation of quality of life is perilous. Some
of these perils are worth noting:

(a) It might mean, in general, that the sufferer's experiences fall
below some standard that the speaker considers desirable. But in
each case the experience in question is different; it can be pain
(the standard being a pain-free existence), loss of mobility, presence of multiple debilitating health problems, loss of mental capacity and of the enjoyment of human interaction, loss of joy in
life, and so on. Poor quality of life, then, refers to many quite
different circumstances.

(b) The judgment of poor quality of life may be made by the one
who lives the life or by an observer. It often happens that lives
which observers consider of poor quality are lived quite satisfac-
torily by the one living that life. Human beings are amazingly
adaptive. They can make the best of the options available. For example, the quadriplegic gymnastics instructor may be a person of
extraordinary motivation; the blind artist may enjoy a vivid imag-
ination; the retarded person may experience simple pleasures.
Thus, when the person's own evaluation is not or cannot be
known to others, those others should be extremely cautious in ap-
plying their own values.

(c) Evaluation of the quality of life, like life itself, changes over
time. The artist's concern may arise from a temporary depression
that will resolve as she discovers her future possibilities; the gymnastics instructor may become deeply depressed. Thus, providers
of care must take care not to make momentous decisions on the
basis of possibly transitory conditions.

(d) The evaluation may reflect bias and prejudice. When sufferers
from mental retardation are said to have "poor quality of life,"
this may reflect our cultural bias in favor of intelligence and productivity. Prejudice may incline some to judge that persons of
such a race, social status or sexual preference cannot possibly live
"good quality" life.

(e) The evaluation may reflect socioeconomic conditions rather than the experienced life of the patient, for example, the lack of home care, of rehabilitation, or special education. These obstacles, while very real, can often be overcome—usually by the ingenuity of social workers.

"Quality of life," then, has a variety of uses. Yet the term often appears in medical literature and in clinical discussions as if it could be used in a simple, unequivocal way. Thus, physicians should be vividly aware of the variety of uses and the possibility for ambiguity and prejudice. When the term is introduced into a discussion, several questions should be asked: Who is making the evaluation? What aspect of life is under consideration? What standard is being used? What are the possibilities for change in the condition? In particular, it is crucial to make explicit the biases of those making the judgment.

3.1.2 **Grading.** Although such adjectives as "high" and "low," "acceptable" and "unacceptable" are used to describe quality of life, such grading is very problematic. If a person says his or her own life is "acceptable," the standards are the person's own; if an onlooker says of another's life, "it is unacceptable," the standards are those of the onlooker, who *presumes* the other would not find a life of that sort acceptable. Furthermore, given the many elements that might make a life satisfactory to an individual, it seems impossible to find common measures or scales for grading. However, some human situations do seem so bad that they would be universally rejected. No one would choose them if the choice were offered. Those who suffer them do so unwillingly or must summon up the greatest heroism. Extreme physical pain, deterioration of motor capacities and loss of control over one's body, profound impairment of mental functioning, incessant and deep emotional turmoil are a few of the human situations that might, with some justification be evaluated as contributing to lessened or low quality of life.

3.1.3 **Subjective Evaluation by Onlooker.** Among the many meanings and uses of the phrase "quality of life," we choose to use the phrase to refer to *subjective evaluation by an onlooker about another's life, when the other is unable to make such an evaluation or express it because of mental incapacity.* We select this usage because it is the one that usually seems to be at issue in crucial ethical deliberations about patient care. In this book *"poor quality"* refers to the existence of severe deficits of physical health, mental health, or social interaction. The phrase *"minimal quality"* refers to situations in which general physical condition has deteriorated beyond recovery and in which interaction between the patient and others is severely restricted. The phrase *"below the threshold considered minimal"* refers to extreme physical debilitation and a complete loss of sensory and intellectual activity. Making these distinctions and referring them to some clinical situations *implies nothing* about how these distinctions should be used as justifications for decisions. Use of these distinctions is discussed in the following paragraphs.

3.2   QUALITY OF LIFE AND TERMINATION OF LIFE SUPPORT

Quality-of-life discussions often take place in situations where an ethical decision must be made about continuing life-supporting interventions. *These situations involve a patient who is not able to express personal preferences at all or whose expression is indiscernible or indecipherable as a result of illness and whose physical condition is critical. In addition, physicians suspect that, if some suggested intervention succeeds, the patient will survive, but with severe deficits of physical or mental capacity.* The question then is asked, "Is such a life worth living?" In this sense, raising the issue of quality of life seems equivalent to wondering whether no life at all is better than a life with certain deficits. This is a metaphysical question, but physicians faced with such decisions seldom enjoy the leisure for metaphysical speculation. The following sections suggest some considerations appropriate to clinical decisions of this sort.

> CASE I.   Mr. CARE (1.4), suffering from advanced MS, has a respiratory arrest associated with gram-negative pneumonia and septicemia. He is placed on a respirator. Within 1 week a neurology consultant states that Mr. CARE has the neurologic signs consistent with chronic vegetative state [1.7.1]. At no time in the course of his care has he expressed any clear preferences about his future. Should respirator support be continued?

COMMENT. (a) Mr. CARE is not brain dead in the proper sense of having lost all function of both higher and lower brain. He still has brain stem activity, respiration, and heartbeat. Thus, he is not legally dead. [See 1.7.]

(b) Medical interventions promise no benefit beyond sustaining organic life. [See 1.5.]

(c) All the functions usual to human interaction and, to the best of the observer's knowledge, all forms of cognitive and sensory experience are absent or extremely deficient. It is extremely unlikely that any of these functions will be recovered.

(d) Note how this case differs from 1.4.4d, in which Mr. CARE is dead according to brain criteria, and 1.4.4a, in which his death is imminent. In those situations the judgment that further intervention is entirely useless, in terms of achieving medical goals, justifies the decision to discontinue mechanical support. In this case Mr. CARE is neither dead nor imminently dying. If respirator support is continued, he will not recover from his disease, nor will he return to mental functioning sufficient for communication. His life, supported by mechanical means, will consist of vegetative activities alone (as far as can be known). On the other hand, if respirator support is removed, Mr. CARE may breathe on his own and continue to live in persistent vegetative state. Life in a vegetative state seems to the physician and the family a life of low —indeed, of no—quality. Their hope is that, once the respirator is discontinued, Mr. CARE will die quickly as the result of his fatal and long disease.

COUNSEL. In our judgment it is ethically permissible to discontinue respiratory support. We argue that the conjunction of three features of this case justifies such a decision. (1) We propose that the state of an irreversible loss of human cognitive and communicative function implies that a "person" no longer exists in any significant sense of the term. This individual is no longer aware of self in relation to surroundings and never will be again. In our terms life has fallen irretrievably below the threshold considered minimal. (2) As a result, no goals of medicine other than support of organic life are being or will be accomplished. We do not believe this goal, in and of itself, is an independent and overriding goal of medicine. (3) Furthermore, it is difficult to know what "benefit" might mean when the patient now, and never will, be able to appreciate what is being done for him or her. (4) No preferences of the patient are expressed or known. The conjunction of these four factors justifies, in our judgment, a decision not to continue medical intervention—that is, physicians have no ethical obligation to continue treatment. Since it is the duty of physician's to benefit their patients, in the absence of benefit, there is no duty to treat. The same argument does not, in and of itself, justify active euthanasia. This is a more complicated question discussed under the heading Euthanasia. [See 3.3.]

2.1 **Withholding or Withdrawing** It is sometimes suggested that there is an ethical difference between withholding an intervention and withdrawing an intervention already begun.

> CASE II. Mr. CARE is in the same condition as described above in Case I. However, he is not on a respirator. He now becomes anuric and is in renal failure. Should dialysis be initiated?

COMMENT. There is no significant ethical difference between Case I and Case II; from the point of view of medical goals, of patient preference, and of assessment of quality of life, the situation is the same. This version, however, involves an instance of not starting an intervention rather than stopping one already being used. Many interventions are initiated at times when their use is quite rational: The achievement of important goals is still seen as possible. When these goals cannot be achieved, and when there are other important considerations, for example, absence of patient preference and quality of life below the minimal threshold, they may be discontinued. In other situations the question is raised whether to initiate another intervention, in face of a new problem, or as a "last ditch stand." *It is our position that there is no significant ethical difference between stopping and not starting, if the essential considerations regarding medical indications, patient preference, and quality of life are the same.*

There may be psychological or emotional differences: Some physicians find it more troubling to stop an ongoing intervention than not to initiate a new one. The initiation of treatment expresses some measure of hope and assuages the uncertainty that plagues clinical medicine. If, despite the physician's efforts, the patient succumbs to the disease, the physician has tried and done his best. However, in withdrawing or stopping treatment, the physician seems to concede defeat. In stopping life-supporting treatment, the physician may feel responsible (in a causal sense) for the events that follow, even though he may bear no responsibility (in the sense of ethical or legal accountability) either for the disease process or for the patient's succumbing to the disease.

Finally, after deciding to refrain from aggressive therapeutic efforts, new medical problems, such as infection or renal failure, sometimes tempt physicians to initiate therapeutic interventions to deal with these particular problems. This is, of course, irrational, unless the intervention has as its purpose another goal more appropriate to the situation, such as providing comfort to the dying patient. [See 1.6.6.; 3.4.]

3.2.2 **Poor Quality of Life.** In the above cases [3.2] Mr. CARE's condition, a persistent vegetative state, represents a quality of life falling below what we have called the "threshold considered minimal." In such situations, the ethical justification for refraining from medical intervention seems to us quite strong. However, in other cases, quality of life, although an important consideration, is a more problematic ethical justification for a decision to refrain from intervention.

CASE I.   Mr. B. B. is 94 years old and living in a nursing home. He sits all day in a chair, without responding to any human attention. He is difficult to feed, frequently choking and expelling food. He has been treated several times in the past month for aspiration pneumonia with antibiotics and fluids. During the night he develops a violent cough and wheezing. He has a fever of 100. The visiting physician diagnoses aspiration pneumonia. Should Mr. B. B. be treated again? [See 1.4–1.4.4.]

CASE II.   Mrs. A. W., a 44-year-old woman, married with three children, has had a long history of scleroderma and ischemic ulcerations of fingers and toes. She is admitted with signs of renal failure. The big toe of her right foot and several fingers of her left hand become gangrenous. Several days later she consents to amputation of the right foot and the thumb and first finger of her left hand. After surgery she is alternately obtunded and confused. She develops pneumonia and is placed on a respirator. The remaining fingers of her left hand become gangrenous and more extensive amputation is required. Her renal condition worsens, and it is now necessary to consider initiating dialysis. The attending says, "How could anyone want to live a life of such terrible quality?" Should the respirator be discontinued? Should dialysis be initiated? [See 1.4–1.4.4.]

COMMENT.   In Mr. B. B.'s case, quality of life refers to the observer's assessment in view of low levels of physical and mental activity. Nothing is known about Mr. B. B.'s own subjective experience. Similarly, the severe physical deficits and the problems of rehabilitation faced by Mrs. A. W. evoke in the observer an assessment that "no one would want to live that way." This, of course, cannot be verified by Mrs. A. W. at this time. There is a difference that is ethically relevant. Mr. B. B. will suffer recurring episodes of aspiration. Even tube feeding might not resolve this problem. Thus, after several episodes it is ethically permissible to refrain from treatment of pneumonia, permitting this disease to be, as it was once called, "the old man's friend." Quality of life, then, has become a relevant consideration, but only insofar as it refers to an objective state, particularly the inability to control motor activities and to cooperate with care in any way. Mr. B. B.'s chronological age is not, in itself, a reason to refrain from treating; only insofar as his chronological age correlates with this physiological state does it become relevant. This objective state makes achievement of medical goals increasingly impossible at the same time medical problems continue to arise.

In contrast, Mrs. A. W. has multiple problems, but all are potentially reversible, with the exception of the loss of extremities. Achievement of significant medical goals is possible. In addition, she herself has consented to the initial amputations, suggesting her willingness to live with these deficits. Finally, her vital personality prior to her surgery suggested to the staff that she had the ability to cope with rehabilitation and the difficulties of subsequent life.

COUNSEL.   In our opinion it is ethically permissible to refrain from treating Mr. B. B.'s pneumonia after several episodes have shown this to be the beginning of a recurring pattern. There is no obligation to proceed with measures such as gastrostomy or gastrogavage. On the other hand, it is ethically obligatory to continue to treat Mrs. A. W.

3.2.3 **Nutrition and Hydration.** Mr. CARE [3.2, Case I] has been started on intravenous fluids and nutrients. Is it permissible to discontinue these measures after he is judged to be in persistent vegetative state? Mr. B. B. [3.2.1, Case I] has deteriorated mentally and now lies in fetal position, showing no response to verbal or tactile stimuli. Should a nasogastric tube be employed? In both cases, death would ensue from starvation and dehydration unless artificial means are used. Is there any special obligation to employ these measures that distinguishes them from respiratory support or medication?

COMMENT.   Some authors argue that feeding is so basic a human function and so symbolic of care that it constitutes "ordinary means" and should never be foregone. Others propose that this measure, like all others, should be judged in view of the balance of benefit over burdens in the patient's experience and that, in certain cases, it is ethically correct to discontinue artificially administered nutrients and even hydration.

COUNSEL.   It is ethically correct to forego nutrients and hydration in Mr. CARE's case. He is in persistent vegetative state and, presumably, lacks all experience. He can neither be benefited nor burdened. In Mr. B. B.'s case, opinion is divided. While profoundly demented, he may still be capable of experience. Some ethicists judge that the burdens of a continual life of pain, discomfort, immobility, dimmed consciousness, and loss of communication would not be desired by any human and that burden so overwhelms benefits of life that there is no obligation to assist in sustaining life. Others wonder about the pain of death by starvation and pause before the social implications of a policy that would deprive the most helpless of basic human attention. Given the diversity of opinion, we judge that either position is ethically permissible. There is also some legal basis for both. [See 3.2.6.]

3.2.4 **Quality-of-Life Judgments and Mental Retardation or Mental Illness.** Quality-of-life judgements are sometimes made about persons whose lives are limited as a result of mental retardation or mental illness. Given the range of possibilities for social intercourse, intellectual achievement, personal accomplishment, and productivity open to most human beings, these persons seem severely restricted. It might be said, then, that they live a life of poor or low quality [in the sense of definitions (b) and (c) in 3.1.3]. When decisions about medical care are made for such persons, is such quality of life a relevant consideration?

> CASE III. Mr. A. S. is a 67-year-old man who has been institutionalized for mental retardation since the age of 1 year. His mental age is estimated at less than the 3-year-old level, and his IQ is 20. He develops acute nonlymphoblastic leukemia. His guardian says, "His life is of such poor quality. Why should we try to extend it?" [See 1.3–1.3.3.]

COMMENT. The above case recalls an actual one in which an important legal decision was rendered (see 3.2.7). The court approved a decision not to treat Mr. Saikewicz with chemotherapy. However, the court attempted to distinguish between the quality of life of retarded persons, which it did not consider relevant to the decision, and the quality of life that Joseph Saikewicz "was likely to experience" under treatment. Speaking of the continued state of pain and disorientation likely to result from chemotherapy, the courts said, "He would experience fear without the understanding from which other patients draw strength." This distinction suggests a point of great ethical importance. Deciding to withhold medical treatment from an individual because that individual belongs to a *class* of persons whose lives are limited in view of social norms for accomplishment and productivity is ethically perilous. It looks more to the burden these persons place on society than to the burden these persons might be to themselves.

The *Saikewicz* court, like all courts that have dealt with such cases, wishes to avoid this argument. The court's reasoning is an attempt to rely on the autonomy of the patient (Chapter 2). It proposes that Mr. A. S., as an individual person, might prefer not to be treated if he experienced the adverse effects of chemotherapy without being able to understand why. In addition, the considerations of Chapter 1 are reflected in the judgment that the likelihood of remission in Mr. A. S.'s case is extremely low. Thus, the court tries to tailor the decision to Mr. A. S. as an individual and allows an assessment of the pain and suffering that he personally will experience to become a decisive consideration. The decision warns against considering Mr. A.S. merely as a member of a class of persons of "poor quality life." If poor quality of life is relevant, it is not the "poor quality" that observers see in the daily existence of a retarded person. It is the life of pain and suffering without understanding that A. S. will experience during chemotherapy (together with a low chance of remission) which constitutes poor quality. A peril of seeing persons as class members for the purpose of medical treatment is the "slippery slope," that is, starting a process in which classes of "undesirables" grow increasingly wider and sweep in more and more persons who are "burdens to themselves and others." This argument is discussed under the heading Euthanasia [3.3].

3.2.5   **The Distasteful Patient.**   There are persons in need of medical care whose manner of life and behavior are extremely distasteful to those who must care for them. They arouse quite negative feelings, which are often expressed in "quality-of-life" terms. True, from many points of view their lives are of "poor quality." Should quality-of-life judgments be relevant to decisions about their treatment? [See 2.8.2–2.8.3.]

> CASE IV.   Mr. C. D. is an alcoholic who inhabits building excavations. He is extremely filthy, foul-mouthed, and, at times, violent and disruptive. He appears quite regularly at the hospital in need of various sorts of care for pneumonia, frostbite, delirium tremens, and so forth. One of the house officers, despite a reprimand from the chief resident, persists in calling him Gomer the Gopher. He is brought to the ER for the third time in a month with bleeding esophageal varices. The ER intern says, "High quality of life like C.'s we can do without." [See 1.3–1.3.3, 1.4–1.4.4.]

> COMMENT.   Mr. C. D.'s quality of life, while certainly low in terms of the objective values of our culture, is not relevant to medical decisions. The question of the burden he imposes on others may be relevant. This is considered in 2.8.3, 4.4, and 4.5.

3.2.6   **Legal Implications.**   The death of a patient resulting from a decision to discontinue medical intervention on the grounds mentioned in 3.2, and 3.2.3. has legal implications. In the cases described in these sections, the patient could be kept alive, perhaps for some time, by continued use of the respirator, by dialysis, or in some other way. It is the "quality" of that continued life that leads to the decision to cease intervention. In contrast, the cases mentioned in 1.5 involved persons whose death was imminent and for whom further intervention was judged useless in terms of medical goals. These latter cases are not likely to generate legal problems unless someone, such as a relative or another physician, claims the judgment of medical uselessness was wrongly made or not made with due care. Cases where quality of life is the central issue, are more legally problematic: A person who *could* be kept alive is allowed to die. In legal theory this might be considered homicide (although the traditional definitions of homicide certainly did not envision the problems occasioned by modern medical technology). The physician might be accused of murder, criminal negligence, or named as an accomplice in the illegal decision of another if he or she accedes to or does not object to the discontinuing of life support by another. To our knowledge physicians have been criminally prosecuted in only one case of this sort [see *Barber v. Superior Court*, 3.2.7]. Nevertheless, fear of such possibilities, coupled with conservative legal advice, often causes physicians to hesitate in making decisions of this sort. However, in several important legal cases, courts have given approval to decisions to withhold or terminate life support. The Karen Ann Quinlan case was the first of these. The legal arguments in these cases are complex and controversial. Although the courts have been reluctant to base decisions on "quality-of-life" grounds, the legal perplexities are being resolved to some extent.

COUNSEL.   In cases of this sort, it is our opinion that physicians are acting within the law, as currently understood, when they decide to withhold or withdraw life-supporting interventions. The conditions required for this decision are: (1) It is virtually certain that further medical intervention will not attain any of the goals of medicine other than sustaining organic life, (2) the preferences of the patient are not known and cannot be expressed, (3) quality of life clearly falls below the threshold considered minimal, (4) family and members of the staff are in accord. We hold this opinion because, despite the legal perplexities, the leading cases thus far adjudicated have affirmed the legal correctness of allowing the patient to die when these conditions are present. In addition, we consider it advisable for institutions to establish an appropriate review committee for cases that present problems. [See 4.1.5.] Finally, institutions should request their legal counsels to prepare clear instructions for the medical staff in view of prevailing local law.

3.2.7.	**Judicial Decisions.**	The most important judicial decisions relevant to cases of this sort are summarized below. These summaries are very brief and, given the legal complexities, may be misleading. They are here stated only to familiarize the reader with the names of the cases and the principal issue.

JUDICIAL DECISIONS RELATING TO LIFE-SUPPORTING INTERVENTIONS

In the Matter of Shirley Dinnerstein, 380 N.E.2d 134 (Mass. Appeals Ct 1978) [upheld validity of "no-code" order on 67-year-old woman suffering from Alzheimer's disease and ruled that such orders did not need court approval].

Application of Eichner [Fox], 426 N.Y.S.2d 517 (decision of New York Supreme Court Appellate Division, Second Judicial Dept, decided March 27, 1980), affirming 423 N.Y.S.2d 580 (Sup Ct, Nassau County, Special Term, Part VI, 1979) [trial court authorized guardian of 83-year-old religious brother in "irreversible vegetative state" to request that respirator be discontinued, based on evidence of patient's prior wishes; appellate court affirmed and laid out procedures to be followed in future cases].

In re Quinlan, 355 A.2d 647 (N.J. Supreme Ct 1976) [authorized discontinuance of life-support system for 21-year-old comatose woman in permanent vegetative state, based on her constitutional right of privacy as asserted by her parents on her behalf; required prior review by a hospital ethics committee].

Superintendent of Belchertown State School v. Saikewicz, 370 N.E.2d 417 (Mass. Supreme Ct 1977) [affirmed trial court decision to not order chemotherapy on 67-year-old severely retarded and institutionalized man suffering from acute myeloblastic leukemia, also on right to privacy grounds, but stressed the role of courts in reviewing such questions].

In the Matter of Spring, 405 N.E.2d 115 (Mass. Sup. Jud. Ct 1980), reversing 399 N.E.2d 493 (Mass. Ct of Appeals 1979) and remanding the judgment to the trial court for further hearings [upheld right of 77-year-old man (who subsequently died in April 1980 during these proceedings) who was senile and suffered from kidney disease to stop hemodialysis treatment; the Supreme Court emphasized that this was not

JUDICIAL DECISIONS RELATING TO LIFE-SUPPORTING INTERVENTIONS (*Continued*)

a decision to be delegated to the attending physician and the man's wife and son, but rather must be made by the probate court on appropriate findings].

Barber v. Superior Court, 147 Cal. App. 3d 1006 (Cal. Appellate Ct 1983) [the court ruled that not only may a respirator be removed from an irreversibly comatose patient but also it is permissible in certain circumstances to discontinue fluids and nutrition. A medical determination that it would be appropriate to withdraw such life support must be made in each case. The incompetent patient's guardian or next-of-kin may then authorize the withdrawal].

Bartling v. Superior Court, 163 Cal. App. 3rd 186 (Cal. Appellate Court 1984) [Mr. William Bartling, a 70-year-old man suffering from multiple chronic, serious illnesses, sought to have a ventilator disconnected even though he knew that he could not survive without it. Despite his explicit request in a written declaration, an explicit verbal request, a "living will," and a Durable Power of Attorney granted to his wife who was willing to carry out his demand, the hospital where Mr. Bartling was a patient refused to comply. Although Mr. Bartling died before this court ruled, it held that competent adult patients have a right, based on the Constitutional right of privacy, to refuse medical treatment. The right to have life-support equipment disconnected is not limited to comatose, terminally ill patients, or representatives acting on their behalf].

In Re Conroy, 486 A. 2d 1209 (New Jersey Sup. Ct., 1985) [the legal guardian for an 84-year-old severely demented woman sought to have all life-sustaining medical treatment, including feeding tubes, withdrawn. The court ruled that all life-sustaining treatment may be withdrawn from incompetent patients provided that is what the patient prefers or would have preferred. The court also ruled that life-sustaining treatment may be withdrawn if it would be in the incompetent patient's best interest, that is, the pain and suffering of continued existence outweigh the benefits derived from prolonged life].

.2.8 **Conclusions.** (a) Quality of life may be considered as decisive in a clinical decision to withhold or withdraw interventions necessary for life when the following conditions are all present:

(i) The indications for medical treatment are such that the goal of preservation of organic life without attainment of the other goals of medicine is likely to be the only accomplishment. [See 1.1.3–1.1.5.]

(ii) The preferences of the patient are not and cannot be known. [See 2.1–2.2.5.]

(iii) The quality of life of the patient falls below threshold that can, on the basis of wide and objective criteria, be considered minimal. [See 3.1.5–3.2.]

In cases where all these conditions are not fulfilled, poor quality of life should not be a decisive consideration. Indeed, it should be suspect; the sorts of judgments that healthy, intelligent, socially accomplished, and technically skilled persons make about the ill, incompetent, or uneducated and unskilled are very likely to be biased. In addition, differences of social and economic class can lead to widely different views of what constitutes a tolerable quality of life. All sorts of "unacceptables" can be swept into the category of persons living lives of poor quality: hippies, gypsies, the uneducated and illiterate, persons of low intelligence or with physical handicaps, those of unfamiliar cultural backgrounds or racial origins disfavored by the majority, and so on. Persons adjudged to fall into these vague categories may no longer be seen as "deserving help." This opens the way to invidious and destructive social policy and violates the ancient medical traditions that help be offered to all in need. Thus, quality-of-life considerations, although often relevant, sometimes important, and on quite specific occasions decisive, should be viewed very cautiously when invoked to justify an ethical decision about whether medical treatment should be provided.

3.3   **EUTHANASIA**

Quality of life and quality of death may be associated: Patients who are in severe pain during terminal disease certainly are living what would appear to be a life of poor quality. It may occur to them or to others that they would be "better off dead." The term "euthanasia," meaning "good death," sometimes appears in this context. (EB: DEATH AND DYING, EUTHANASIA AND SUSTAINING LIFE.)

3.3.1   **Definition.**   The word "euthanasia" is used in many different ways, resulting in considerable confusion. In the popular sense, it refers to mercy killing, for example, deliberately administering a lethal drug to a sufferer. Philosophers and, to some extent, physicians attempt to use the word with more exact meaning, even though there is little agreement about what that meaning is. They distinguish between "voluntary and involuntary," "active and passive." Similarly, the terms "omission and commission," or "acting and withholding" are sometimes used. The definitions of all these terms are much debated. Even if they were clearly defined, merely using the right words would not make one decision ethical and another unethical. We note those clinical situations where certain of these terms are likely to be used. Thus, the situations described in 1.5, in which a decision is taken to withdraw or withhold medical interventions of little utility, may be called "passive euthanasia." Some call situations described in 2.5, in which patients refuse interventions that will keep them alive, "voluntary euthanasia." Others wish to reserve voluntary euthanasia only for situations in which patients request that their life be ended by a lethal act. When the quality of a persons's life is so compromised by pain and/or debilitation that a physician might be asked to kill the patient directly, the term "active euthanasia" might be used.

3.2 **"Active Euthanasia."** "Active euthaniasia" sometimes describes the situation in which someone (perhaps a physician) administers some lethal agent, e.g., a bolus of air, potassium chloride IV, excessive barbiturates, with the intention of causing the cessation of organic functions necessary to life.

> CASE I. Mr. CARE is now suffering from advanced MS. He is bedridden, almost totally helpless and obtunded. His wife and brother ask his doctor to give him something to end his life.

> CASE II. Ms. T. O. is dying from widely disseminated cancer and is suffering intense and implacable pain. She begs her doctor "to put her to sleep forever."

3.3 **Moral Prohibitions.** Active intervention to cause or hasten death, whether done by a physician or by another, faces very strong moral prohibitions in our culture:

(a) Prohibition of the direct taking of human life, except in self-defense or in the defense of others, has been a central tenet of the Judeo-Christian tradition. It has been equally strong in the secular ethic.

(b) The ethics of medicine has traditionally emphasized the saving and preservation of life and has repudiated the direct taking of life. The Hippocratic Oath states, "I will not administer poison to anyone when asked to do so nor suggest such a course."

(c) The dedication of the medical profession to the welfare of patients and to the promotion of their health might be seriously undermined in the eyes of the public and of patients by the complicity of physicians in the death of the very ill.

(d) Even in particular cases, when effecting a swift death at the request of a suffering patient seems merciful and benevolent, the acceptance of the practice as ethical may bear the seeds of frightening social consequences. The "angel of mercy" can become the fanatic, bringing the "comfort" of death to some who do not so clearly request it, then to others who "would really be better off dead," finally to classes of "undesirable persons." The "euthanasia" program initiated in Germany in the early 1930s with the support of many benevolent physicians was first directed only to the incurably ill; it gradually expanded into genocide.

(e) Requests for swift death are often made in circumstances of extreme distress, which may be alleviated by skillful pain management and other positive interventions such as those developed by the Hospice movement. [See 3.4.]

COUNSEL.   These arguments appear to many commentators to add up to a decisive conclusion: Physicians have an ethical obligation to refrain from active euthanasia. Other commentators are not so absolute. They suggest that active euthanasia may be permissible in certain very restricted circumstances. Should any physician come to the conclusion that he should accede to the plea of a sufferer who requests death, such a decision, however conscientious, entails serious moral and legal perils. [On infant euthanasia, see 5.3.3.]

3.3.4   **"Death with Dignity."**   The phrase "death with dignity" is sometimes heard in discussions of allowing to die and causing death. While appealing, the phrase is ambiguous and should not be allowed to carry weight in ethical deliberations without a precise definition of its meaning. If it is intended to mean that the expressed preferences of patients to refuse further medical intervention should be respected, "death with dignity" has important ethical significance: It is respect for the autonomy of the dying person. If it is intended to mean that dying persons should be spared the pain and inconvenience of repeated interventions of little utility, it also has ethical significance: It refers to the ethical obligation to shift from aggressive therapy to comforting care when therapy is futile. However, if it is intended to say that the suffering patient should be put "out of misery," it is ethically questionable and can be criticized by all of the arguments mentioned above. The phrase "death with dignity" should be reserved to describe the obligation to care for the dying sensitively, compassionately, and ethically.

.3.5 **Legal Implications.** Deliberately causing the death of another constitutes a criminal act, as does cooperating in the causing of another's death. Thus, the physician who administers or provides a lethal agent is liable to a criminal charge of homicide or assisting suicide. Decisions to allow persons who are terminally ill to die, discussed in the previous chapters and sections, are also examples of "causing" the death of another. However, the clinical decision that further medical care would provide no therapeutic benefit other than to prolong organic life relieves the physician of the legal duty to continue to intervene with medical measures. This has long been considered an adequate defense against criminal and civil charges. A decision to kill the patient by using some lethal agent, even when death is imminent, does not rest on a clinical judgment about the futility of medical care. It is a decision that can be made by persons without medical skills, and the lethal agent can be a bullet, an electric shock, or rat poison. The "merciful" intent of the perpetrator is not a defense recognized by the law. In such situations, anyone who kills another human being can be charged with a criminal offense. Physicians and laypersons alike must stand before the law.

3.4 **PAIN RELIEF**

In clinical situations a determination that the case is hopeless may lead to a decision to terminate life support. At the same time the patient may be conscious and in severe pain. Medication for pain relief is appropriate. Should it be provided up to the point where respiratory capacity is compromised, leading to death? It is clear that relief of pain is one of the major goals of medicine. It responds to the expressed preferences of the patient. It also improves the quality of life for the patient. On all these points, it is ethical. What is unclear is whether the side effect of analgesic medication, respiratory failure, should be considered as equivalent to active euthanasia.

3.4.1 **Skilled Use of Pain Medication.** This problem can be avoided by intelligent and skilled use of pain medication. Unfortunately, intelligent and skilled use of these drugs is less common than could be desired. This lack, however, is increasingly recognized, and literature is beginning to appear. Physicians should educate themselves and should seek consultation with persons expert in pharmacology and clinical pharmacy. Patients should not be kept on a regimen inadequate to control pain because of the ignorance of the physician or because of an ungrounded fear of addiction.

3.4.2 **Pain Relief and Maintenance of Compromised Functions.** On occasion, it is difficult to manage pain medication so that palliative effects and depressant effects are balanced. In such situations, should maintenance of adequate respiratory status take precedence over pain relief? Relief of pain and maintenance of compromised function are both goals of medicine. It can be plausibly argued that in the situation of the dying patient, the goal of maintenance of compromised function is itself related to the goal of prolonging life; prolonging life, in turn, is a goal that in this case has been properly abandoned. Thus, relief of pain becomes the primary goal to be sought during the remaining time of the patient's life.

3.4.3 **Double Effect.** The ethics of this problem are sometimes discussed in terms of "double effect." While this ethical thesis has been much criticized, many ethicists find the following arguments acceptable.

Some actions have several effects that are inextricably linked. One of those effects is intended by the agent and is ethically permissible (e.g., relief of pain); the other is not intended by the agent and is ethically questionable (e.g., respiratory depression).

Proponents of this argument state that the ethically permissible effect can be allowed, even if the ethically questionable one will inevitably follow, when the following conditions are present:

(a) The action itself is ethically good or at least indifferent, that is, neither good nor evil in itself (in this case the action is the administration of a drug, a morally indifferent act).

(b) The agent must intend the good effects, not the evil effects, even though these are foreseen (in this case the intention is to relieve pain, not to kill the patient).

(c) The morally objectionable effect cannot be a means to the morally permissible one (in this case death is not the means to relief of pain).

In this argument the major practical problem for the clinician lies with the second condition (b), since often the intention of the physician is mixed; to relieve pain and to hasten death. If it can be said that the dosages administered are clinically rational, that is, no more drug is administered than is necessary for adequate pain relief, the intention to relieve pain seems primary and the action is ethical. If doses in excess of clinical necessity are given, the intention to hasten death seems primary. If this latter intention becomes primary, the action would be judged unethical. Roman Catholic medical ethics employs this argument to justify clinically appropriate pain medication for relief of pain, even if the unintended foreseen effect is the hastening of the patient's death. (EB: DOUBLE EFFECT.)

> EXAMPLE. A 56-year-old woman suffers from carcinoma of the breast with lymphangitic spread to lungs and bony metastases. She requires increasing narcotic dosage for relief of pain. Her pulmonary function deteriorates so that her pO_2 is 45 and pCO_2 is 55 when she is pain-free. [See 1.4–1.4.4.]

COMMENT. Respiratory depression is the probable side effect of appropriate dosages of morphine (i.e., sufficient to relieve pain). It is "unintended" in the sense that, if pain could be relieved by other means which would not have the effect, those means would be preferred.

3.4.4   **Diminution of Consciousness and Communication.**   Attempts to achieve adequate relief of pain have another side effect, namely, the clouding of the patient's consciousness and the hindering of the patient's communication with family and friends. This double effect may be ethically troubling to the physician and to nurses. In such situations no ethical principle will resolve the problem. Rather, sensitive attention to the patient's needs, together with skilled medical management, should lead as close as possible to the desired objective: maximum relief of pain with minimal diminution of consciousness and communication. Of course, if the patient is able to express preferences, these should be followed.

3.4.5   **Fear of Addiction.**   It is common that patients are not medicated adequately because providers fear this may induce addiction. This fear is irrational in the situation when death is imminent. Inadequate medication should be considered as unethical as overmedication.

3.4.6   **Physiological, Psychological, Social, and Spiritual Components.**   Relief of pain is complex; it has physiological, psychological, social, and spiritual components. Attempts to deal with one factor alone in this complex network will often be futile. Thus, concentration on the physiologic components of pain through pharmacologic or surgical interventions, without equal attention to the psychological, social, and spiritual, may bring little relief. Even if relief is achieved in the physiologic sense, other important ethical responsibilities may be left unfulfilled, for example, aiding patients to deal with their death and its effect on others. Physicians should make themselves aware of these components and seek assistance from those expert in dealing with them. The presence of religious counselors is often of immeasurable value to the patient, to the family, and to the physician.

3.5   **SUICIDE**

Suicide is the deliberate taking of one's own life. As an ethical problem, it should be discussed under Patient Preferences in Chapter 2. However, since the physician will often encounter the problem either at the end of the terminal illness of a patient, when life is of "poor quality," or in the Emergency Room, when preferences can only be inferred, it is discussed here. (EB: SUICIDE.)

There are significant ethical differences between suicide and the refusal of treatment:

(a) In refusal of care, persons do not take their lives; rather they do not permit another to help them survive. Persons who abhor the thought of suicide may say, "I do not want to kill myself. I only want to be allowed to die."

(b) In refusal of care, death is imminent from an irreversible disease; in suicide, although there may be irreversible disease, death is effected by some other self-inflicted lethal act. In refusing life-saving care the patient does not set in motion the lethal cause; the fatal condition is itself the cause of death.

(c) Even though the result of suicide and refusal is the same, death, the moral setting differs completely in intention, circumstances, motives, and desires.

(d) The Roman Catholic Church, which adamantly condemns suicide, does permit its adherents to refuse care, even should death result, when treatment offers little hope and is burdensome, painful, or costly ("extraordinary"). [See 2.6.1.]

(e) Many judicial decisions and legal statutes now distinguish between legitimate refusal of care and suicide.

3.5.1 **Legal Considerations.** Anglo-American law long maintained sanctions against suicide. Suicides were punished by disinheritance of survivors and burial in unconsecrated ground; attempted suicides were considered felons. In the current century, laws against suicide were repealed in all states. The law now forbids assisting in a suicide. Physicians should refrain from assistance in suicide for the same reasons stated in 3.3.3 (active euthanasia).

3.5.2 **Treatment of Suspected Suicides.** Suspected suicides are frequently encountered in the emergency room. Even when the suspicion is supported by evidence, such as history and a suicide note, it has been customary to provide all means necessary for resuscitation and care, if there are solid medical grounds to expect recovery.

> CASE. A 24-year-old woman is brought to the ER; she has deeply slashed her wrists and has overdosed. She has been

brought several times before and is known to have a psychiatric history of depression. On her last admission she screamed that next time she should be allowed to die. [See 1.3–1.3.3.]

COUNSEL. The customary practice of disregarding the suicide wish in the emergency situation seems ethically appropriate, even though it seems to contravene the autonomy of the person.

(a) The ethical basis for suicide prevention is the well-known psychological thesis that the suicide attempt is very often a "cry for help" rather than an unambivalent decision to end one's life. Frequently the very fact that the attempted suicide arrives in the ER suggests the act was ambivalently motivated. Many suicides are made halfway. The suicide attempt may not be an act of autonomy but rather an act resulting from impaired capacity due to some emotional conflict.

(b) Full circumstances surrounding the apparent suicide will rarely be known in the emergency setting. Thus, discrimination between genuine suicides and ungenuine suicides, as well as between suicides and acts of criminal battery, in the urgency of the ER would leave open wide possibilities for error, prejudice, and bias. The apparent suicide may not be a suicide at all.

3.5.3 **Ethical Obligation of the Physician.** Physicians have an ethical obligation to recognize the suicidal inclinations of patients whom they encounter in their practice and to make efforts to assist them personally or by referral to a trained counselor.

BIBLIOGRAPHY

3.–3.1 *Quality of Life and Its Meaning*

Epstein, A., Taylor, W., Seage, G. Effects of patient's socioeconomic status and physician training on patient–doctor communication. Am J Med, 1985, 78:101.

Evans, R., Manninen, P., Garrison, L., et al. Quality of life of patients with end stage renal disease. N Engl J Med, 1985, 212:553.

Fletcher, J. Indicators of humanhood. Hastings Cent Rep, 1972, 2(5):1.

Mack, R. Lessons from living with cancer. N Engl J Med, 1984, 311:1640.

McCormick, R. The quality of life, the sanctity of life. Hastings Cent Rep, 1978, 8:32.

McCormick, R. To save or let die: The dilemma of modern medicine. JAMA, 1974, 229:172.

Prigatano, G., Wright, E., Levin, D., et al. Quality of life and its predictors in patients with mild hypoxemia and chronic obstructive pulmonary disease. Arch Intern Med, 1984, 144:1613.

Pearlman, R., Jonsen A. Use of quality of life considerations in medical decision making. J Am Geriat Soc, 1985, 33:344.

Shaw, A. Defining quality of life. Hastings Cent Rep, 1977, 7(5):11.

Stollerman, G. Quality of life: Treatment decisions and the third alternative. J Am Geriat Soc, 1984, 32:483.

Thomasma, D. Ethical judgments of quality of life in the care of the aged. J Am Geriat Soc, 1984, 32:525.

3.2 *Quality of Life and Termination of Life Support*

Besdine, R. Decisions to withhold treatment from nursing home residents. J Am Geriat Soc, 1983, 31:602.

Brown, N., Thompson, D. Non-treatment of fever in extended care facilities. N Engl J Med, 1979, 300:1246.

Callahan, D. On feeding the dying. Hastings Cent Rep, 1983, 13:22.

Callahan, D. On defining a natural death. Hastings Cent Rep, 1977, 7(3):32.

Dresser, R. S., Boisaubin, E. Ethics, law and nutritional support. Arch Intern Med, 1985, 145:122.

Dyck, A. Ethical aspects of care for the dying incompetent. J Am Geriat Soc, 1984, 32:661.

Hilfiker, D. Allowing the debilitated to die: Facing our ethical choices. N Engl J Med, 1983, 308:716.

Lo, B. The death of Clarence Herbert: Withdrawing care is not murder. Ann Intern Med, 1984, 101:248.

Lo, B., Dorenbrand, L. Guiding the hand that feeds: Caring for the demented elderly. N Engl J Med, 1984, 311:402.

Lynn, J., Childress, J. Must patients always be given food and water? Hastings Cent Rep, 1983; 13:17.

Marina, W. Decision making in the care of terminally ill incompetent persons: Concerns about the role of the courts. J Am Geriat Soc, 1984, 32:739.

Meyers, D *Medicolegal Implications*, Chapter 12. (See General References.)

Meyers, D. Legal aspects of withdrawing nourishment from an incurably ill patient. Arch Intern Med, 1985, 145:125.

Micetich, K., Steinecker, P., Thomasma, D. Are intravenous fluids morally required for a dying patient? Arch Intern Med, 1983, 143:975.

Paris, J., Reardon, F. Court responses to withholding or withdrawing artificial nutrition and fluids. JAMA, 1985, 253:2243.

Rosner, R. Bleich, J. D. *Jewish Bioethics*, Chapters 15-19. (See General References.)

Siegler, M., Weisbard, A. Against the emerging stream: Should fluids and nutritional support be discontinued. Arch Intern Med, 1985, 145:129.

Suckiel, E. J. Death and benefit in the permanently unconscious patients. J Med Philos, 1978, 3:38.

Thomasma, D. Freedom, dependency and the care of the very old. J Am Geriat Soc, 1984, 32:906.

Watts, D., Cassel, C. Extraordinary nutritional support: A case study and ethical analysis. J Am Geriat Soc, 1984, 32:237.

3.3 *Euthanasia*

Alexander, L. Medical science under dictatorship. N Engl J Med, 1949, 241:39.

Baker, R. On euthanasia. In *Biomedical Ethics Review*. J. Humber, R. Almeder (eds). Clifton, N.J.: Humana Press, 1983.

Beauchamp, T. A reply to Rachels on active and passive euthanasia. In *Ethical Issues in Death and Dying*. T. Beauchamp, S. Perlin (eds). Englewood Cliffs, N.J.: Prentice-Hall, 1978.

Beauchamp, T., Davidson A. The definition of euthanasia. J Med Philos, 1979, 4:294.

Biomedical ethics and the shadow of nazism. Hastings Cent Rep, 1976, 6(4)(Suppl).

Foot, P. Euthanasia, Philos Pub Affairs, 1977, 6:85.

Kohl, M. *Beneficent Euthanasia*. Buffalo, N.Y.: Prometheus Books, 1975.

Meier, D., Cassel, C. Euthanasia in old age: A case study and ethical analysis. J Am Geriat Soc, 1983, 31:294-298.

Meyers, D. *Medicolegal Implications*, Chapter 7. (See General References.)

President's Commission for the Study of Ethical Problems in Medicine and Biomedical and Behavioral Research. *Deciding to Forego Life-Sustaining Treatment*. (See General References.)

Ramsey, P. The indignity of death with dignity. Hastings Cent Rep, 1974, 2(2): 47.

3.4 *Pain Relief*

Angell, M. The quality of mercy. N Engl J Med, 1982, 306:98.

Beauchamp, T. L., Childress, J. F. *Principles of Biomedical Ethics*, Chapter 4. (See General References.)

Boyle, J. Toward understanding the principle of double effect. Ethics, 1980, 80:527.

Cassell, E. The relief of suffering. Arch Intern Med, 1983, 143:522.

Graber, G. Some questions about double effect. Ethics Med, 1979, 6:65.

Levine, J. Pain and analgesia: The outlook for more rational treatment. Ann Intern Med, 1984, 100:269.

Marks, R. Sachar, E. Undertreatment of medical inpatients with narcotic analgesics. Ann Intern Med, 1973, 78:173.

McGivney, W., Crooks, G. The care of patients with severe chronic pain in terminal illness. JAMA, 1984, 251:1182.

Saunders, C. *The Management of Terminal Disease*. Chicago: Year Book Medical Publishers, 1979.

Vanderpool, H. Y. The ethics of terminal care. JAMA, 1978, 239:850.

3.5 *Suicide*

Bromberg, A., Cassell, E. Suicide in the elderly: the limits of paternalism. J Am Geriat Soc, 1983, 31:698.

Lebacqz, K., Engelhardt, H. T. Suicide. In *Death, Dying and Euthanasia*. D. J. Horan, D. Mall (eds). Washington, D.C.: University Publications, 1977.

Meyers, D. *Medicolegal Implications*, Chapter 7. (See General References.)

Perlin, S. (ed). *Handbook for the Study of Suicide*. New York and Oxford: Oxford University Press, 1975.

Ruben, H. Managing suicidal behavior. JAMA, 1979, 241:282.

Thorup, O., Siegler, M., Childress, J. Voluntary exit: is there a case for rational suicide. Pharos 1982, 45:25.

4

SOCIOECONOMIC FACTORS

4.0 Medicine has traditionally concentrated on the medical needs of individual persons seeking medical care. The care and cure of individuals are its objectives. Medical care, however, does not take place within the isolation of a one-on-one encounter between patient and physician. Family, friends, institutional arrangements, social structures, cultural values, economic conditions—all these influence the patient–physician relationship. It has also long been recognized that many factors external to the person are important for the understanding and management of the illness and for the promotion of health. However, in the physician's efforts to assist a patient, the interests of persons other than the patient have traditionally played a very limited role.

Still, these factors are ever more compelling, and those making clinical decisions must decide how and to what extent they should influence choice.

The socioeconomic factors discussed in this chapter are (1) the role of interested parties other than the patient, for example, relatives (2) the costs of medical care, (3) the allocation of medical resources, (4) research, (5) medical teaching, and (6) safety and welfare of society. The question raised by these factors is whether, and to what extent, burdens and benefits accruing to persons other than the patient should be relevant or decisive in clinical decisions regarding the patient.

All of the ethical principles previously discussed in this book underlie the problems of this chapter. However, the principle of utilitarianism, that is, those actions are ethically right that contribute to the greater good of the greater number, is particularly relevant. In some of its interpretations, this principle may appear to conflict directly with the duty of a physician to benefit and not to harm the individual patient who is being cared for. Also, ethical doctrines of justice, requiring fair distribution of social benefits, may propose policies that appear incompatible with the physician's duty to individual patients. It is the purpose of this chapter to state some of those situations where clinical benefits and social benefits might appear to dictate different courses of action. It is our opinion that the principle of duty to the patient's welfare should prevail in almost all circumstances. The circumstances in which we favor benefit to others than the patient are stated. If our counsel seems at times somewhat uncertain, it is because some of these situations do pose genuine dilemmas. (EB: ETHICS, UTILITARIANISM, HEALTH POLICY, JUSTICE, SOCIAL MEDICINE.)

4.1 DIFFERENTIATION BETWEEN CLINICAL JUDGMENT AND HEALTH POLICY

It is important to note that this chapter is still about the *clinical judgment* of physicians in managing individual patients. It is *not* about health policy. This chapter's comments are applicable only to the clinical situation. Quite a different framework of thought must be devised to deal with questions of health policy and the ethical issues raised by policy proposals. Even though clinical decisions and policy decisions are related in intricate ways, policy decisions are made in different ways, for different purposes, and in a different atmosphere from clinical decisions. Thus, when a policymaker asks "whether better use for resources exists than [say] neonatal intensive care or Magnetic Resonance Imager," the answer depends upon many facts and considerations not available to the clinician. Further, the policymaker is accountable to the public in a much more visible and definitive way than is the clinician. The physician is accountable to the individual patient and not to the public.

> EXAMPLE.   Mrs. COPE, the noncompliant diabetic [2.8], is now hospitalized for treatment of severe ketoacidosis. Ulcerations on her legs, incurred during a recent alcoholic episode, are not healing. She develops acute renal failure. The Renal Fellow says, somewhat in jest, "We really ought to reduce the burden on the End-Stage Renal Disease Program. Somehow dialysis has to be rationed. We ought to start here."

COMMENT.   The cynical remark of the Fellow would, if taken seriously, substitute a concern about the national policy governing the use of an expensive resource for the interests of the patient who is his responsibility. If the same remark, without reference to any individual patient, was made by the Assistant Secretary for Health, Department of Health and Human Services (DHHS), it would express a legitimate policy concern and might be answered, after extensive study, by devising a program that would be both cost-effective and fair.

The legitimacy of the DHHS officer's remark, in contrast to that of the Renal Fellow, rests on at least three reasons:

(a) The former is a public statement, susceptible to public analysis and criticism; the latter is made in private, providing no opportunity for public scrutiny.

(b) The former would be pursued by determining standards and procedures and specific criteria for inclusion and exclusion of recipients of care; the latter appears to issue from emotion and prejudice, outside any context of standards, procedures, and criteria.

(c) The former represents the role and task of a DHHS officer; the latter in no way represents the role and task of physicians (unless they are also public officials) in our society.

4.1.1 **Creation of Ethical Problems by Institutions and Policies.** Many of the ethical problems raised by clinical decisions about particular patients are caused by social policies and the structure of institutions. For a variety of reasons, such as limited fiscal resources or political pressures, social and institutional policies will favor some groups at the expense of others.

EXAMPLE:　Patients with end-stage renal disease are the object of a public program specially designed for them; patients with hemophilia do not enjoy such a program.

This may lead to clinical decisions about such patients that are forced by the circumstances of social policy and financial resources. Individual physicians may be able to do little about these circumstances. Thus, the physician may be faced with undesirable options for ethical choice. Although we are vividly aware that inequitable, inefficient, or inadequate social policies do create situations where all ethical options are less than ideal, this chapter does not discuss the reform of social policy. This is a problem that must be taken up elsewhere. This chapter deals only with the clinical decisions themselves.

4.1.2　**Relevance of Socioeconomic Factors.**　It is tempting but simplistic to say that socioeconomic factors should never be allowed to influence a decision about a patient: Only the patient's welfare, not the welfare of others, should be the clinician's objective. This is tempting because it reflects the traditional Hippocratic éthic of patient benefit. It is simplistic because holding so absolutely to a principle, in this case as in others, creates situations that appear to almost every rational observer as unethical.

EXAMPLE I.　A physician in 1904 stood by silently while a young man whom he knew to have syphilis married without telling his fiancee his condition. The physician wrote: "A single word would save her from this terrible fate, yet the physician is fettered hand and foot by his cast iron code . . . he cannot lift a finger or utter a word to prevent this catastrophe" (Bok, 1978, p. 147; [2.4] on Confidentiality, see 4.3.).

In certain cases, consideration of another's welfare certainly does not seem unethical, but is still troubling because of the departure from the principle of patient benefit.

EXAMPLE II.　A 72-year-old man who is senile suffers from severe emphysema. He is being cared for, with great difficulty, by his 72-year old wife who is becoming increasingly distraught. Still, she insists she does not want him to go into a nursing home. When the patient develops pneumonia, it occurs to the physician that "his death would certainly be a great relief to his wife." [See 4.2.6.]

Finally, burdens that are distributed broadly through the society may be raised as relevant to the care of a patient.

EXAMPLE III. Should the high costs of the End-Stage Renal Disease Program be relevant to a decision about admitting Mrs. COPE to dialysis? [See 4.1, 4.5.]

.1.3 **Decisiveness of Socioeconomic Factors.** Should burdens that arise from patient care but fall on others ever be decisive in decisions about these patients?

CASE I. The 29-year-old retarded man described in 3.1.1 develops acute lymphoblastic leukemia. His parents are unwilling to continue to carry the burden of his care. They refuse permission for treatment of leukemia. Should the socioeconomic factor, that is, the burden imposed upon the parents, be the decisive consideration in deciding not to treat?

COMMENT. As a general principle, we propose that socioeconomic factors should not be decisive over consideration of (1) medical indications, (2) patient preference, and (3) quality of life. However, socioeconomic factors may move toward greater decisiveness in clinical decisions when all of the following conditions are met:

(a) The achievement of significant goals of medical intervention is doubtful. [See 1.1.3.]

(b) The preferences of the patient are not and cannot be known. [See 2.2.5.]

(c) The quality of the patient's life approaches the threshold considered minimal. [See 3.1.3.]

(d) The socioeconomic factor in question is specific, notably burdensome to others, and the decision will make a difference in alleviating that burden.

COUNSEL. The burden imposed upon the parents of the retarded man is a relevant and important consideration. However, it should not be decisive because (1) significant medical goals can be achieved and (2) the quality of the patient's life, while poor, is not close to the minimal threshold. Chemotherapy is ethically mandatory.

CASE II.   Mrs. C. Z., a 35-year-old woman, has been through several courses of chemotherapy for Hodgkin's disease to no avail. Her tumor is now staged at IVB. She has decided to discontinue chemotherapy and accept only palliative care. While in the hospital for treatment of severe edema of the neck and cellulitis, she chokes on soup and, before an airway can be opened, suffers 5 minutes of anoxia. Two weeks later she is on a respirator and has been described by the neurologists as being in a persistent vegetative state. Her husband insists she be kept alive. The costs of this admission now approach $15,000. Should the respirator be turned off?

COMMENT.   In this case, two factors, the wishes of the husband and the costs of care, deserve consideration. The considerations directly relevant to the patient lead to the following conclusions: (1) The indications for medical intervention bear only on the minimal goal of treatment, namely, preservation of organic life; no other goals are attainable. (2) The preferences of the patient are not known and cannot be ascertained. (3) The quality of her life is at, or below, the threshold considered minimal. (4) If the husband cannot emotionally accept the loss of his wife and insists on continued intervention, it is certainly permissible to continue while attempting to counsel this man. In such a situation, the wishes of her husband, while *important*, are not decisive. The costs of care and the allocation of resources may be decisive. Each of these factors will be discussed in 4.2–4.5.

4.1.4   **External Review of Socioeconomic Factors.**   In the usual course of the practice of medicine, important decisions are, and should be, made by the patient and the physician together. Outside parties have no right to partake in those decisions unless invited to do so by the principal parties. However, when socioeconomic factors become relevant to a particular clinical decision under the circumstances mentioned above, a strong case can be made for the more prominent role of external parties. The presence of socioeconomic factors raises the issue of conflict of interest, since someone other than the patient will bear burdens or enjoy benefits resulting from the decision. One traditional means of preventing conflict of interest from leading to results harmful to one of the principals is review by persons who do not have an interest in the outcome. External review, when appropriate, can provide balance, dispassionate advice, and protection to all parties. Thus, when discussing various external factors, we suggest some sort of external review is often advisable. Common forms of external review are the appointment of guardians or conservators, the judicial proceeding, review committees (such as those now existing for human experimentation), and processes of administrative oversight.

4.1.5   **Medical Ethics Committees.**   In recent years many hospitals have established medical ethics committees. They are useful for consultation regarding complicated cases. Legal, medical, and ethical ramifications of a decision can be explored. Different views regarding prognosis and indications for treatment can be exposed. Arguments about "quality of life" can be closely scrutinized. In particular, conflicts among family members or among the medical and nursing team can be mediated. Committee review may provide assurance that full and impartial consideration has been given to a difficult ethical decision. Committees should be used for consultation and review; they should not be substituted for the responsible decision of the attending physician.

4.2   **ROLE OF INTERESTED PARTIES**

Patients come from a social setting: other persons are related to them, know them, work with them. These persons may have interests in the patient's course and sometimes are deeply involved in decisions about the patient. How is their role to be defined ethically and legally?

4.2.1   **Moral Authority of the Family.**   In American culture, the moral authority of the immediate family is significant, although it is perhaps less dominant than in other cultures. Physicians should pay close attention to family members in situations where the patient is unable to make decisions. Their wishes are ethically *important* primarily because they may reflect the personal preferences of the patient who is, at present, unable to express them. Family may be the best source of information about their relative's preferences, judgments of quality life, and so forth. Since patient preferences are one of the most ethically decisive factors in treatment decisions, any evidence about them is important.

> CASE.   An 83-year old woman suffers extensive chest and pelvic trauma when hit by a car. She is on a respirator in the ICU. She is somewhat confused and disoriented. However, she continues to write notes saying, "I want to die" and "Leave me alone." Her two sons and one daughter arrive from a distant city. They state their mother was a very independent woman until her accident. She is intelligent and well informed. She has said to them many times, "I don't want to be dependent. I don't want to deteriorate. I don't want to be like my sister" (who was severely debilitated by a stroke for 7 years before her death). [See 1.3–1.3.3.]

COMMENT.   The testimony of the sons and daughter is important evidence of their mother's preferences. There is no reason to suspect it is false or to suspect them of ulterior motives. If they had merely said, "She should be allowed to die; she'd be better off dead than deteriorating," they might have been expressing *their* preferences rather than *hers*. The expression by family of the patient's preferences is clearly relevant and may be decisive. The expression of *their own* preferences is less important ethically and may not even be relevant.

4.2.2   **Legal Authority of Family.**   Family members and next of kin have *no legal authority* to make crucial decisions on behalf of *adult* patients unable to make decisions on their own behalf, unless that authority is specifically given by the act of a judge granting guardianship powers (or in several states, by a statute). Parents or guardians do have legal authority by statute to make decisions for minors, with certain limitations. [See 2.7.4.;5.2.]

Physicians *must not assume* they have a legal duty to obtain permission of next of kin to perform medical acts for an incapacitated patient. Physicians should be informed about the exact legal status of next of kin. It is, of course, always advisable to consult with next of kin. In certain situations, it is prudent to recommend that a legal guardianship be obtained by a family member for the specific purpose of making decisions regarding medical care. This should usually be done when there is question of a major intervention, such as elective surgery or embarking on a course of chemotherapy for an incapacitated patient.

In the case of Mrs. C. Z. mentioned above [4.1.5], the husband has no legal authority to determine whether treatment continue or cease. Physicians have no legal duty to act in accord with his wishes. He may seek and be granted such authority after petitioning a judge, who may require a hearing. Other parties, such as her parents or her physician, might also petition for legal guardianship.

4.2.3 **Conflict of Interest.**   Conflict of interest or other sorts of biases in the expressions of family about their ill relatives may be suspected. If the suspicion is well grounded, their statements about their relatives should not be considered relevant to decisions about their care.

> CASE I.   A 76-year-old man is found in his boardinghouse room comatose, hypothermic, emaciated, and with gangrene of toes on both feet. After being taken to the hospital, he is found to be in renal failure. Social workers contact his family, a son and a daughter. The former operates a successful business in a neighboring state; the latter is a prominent local socialite. On arriving at the hospital, they insist that "everything be done to keep their father alive." The daughter expresses surprise that he is so ill since, "while I don't see him very often, I had always told him to get in touch if he needed me." [See 1.4–1.4.4.]

> CASE II.   The same as Case I, with these modifications: The patient, despite living in poverty and isolation, is known to have a considerable fortune. His son and daughter tell you, "You must let him die in peace. His last years have been so miserable."

COMMENT.   In both versions of the case there is reason to suspect the son and daughter are not acting in the best interest of their father. In the first version, guilt over neglect may supply strong self-interested motives; in the second the prospect of inheritance may do so. This does not mean a decision to treat in version I or not to treat in version II would be wrong; it simply means that such a decision should not be based on the wishes of next of kin. Rather, the questions of direct patient welfare, raised in Chapters 2 and 3, are much more important and, in most cases, should be decisive.

COUNSEL.   Family wishes should be considered *important* in clinical decisions about patients unable to express their preferences when (1) there is no reason to suspect bias or conflict of interest, and (2) relatives show evidence of close and continuing concern for the patient.

4.2.4   **Best Interests of the Patient.**   Decisions made by others about the patient should always be in the patient's best interest. [cf. 2.7.1; 5.3.2] Obviously, what constitutes "best interest" may be controversial. Is continued painful treatment with little hope of cure, but with the effect of prolonging life, in the patient's best interest? Is death ever in a person's "best interest"? Determination of best interest, for practical purposes of clinical decisions, should look to the following:

(a) It can be presumed that attainment of the goals of medical intervention would be in the interest of the patient. If significant goals are unlikely to be attained, treatment may not be in the patient's interest. [See 1.1.3.]

(b) If only the minimal goal, maintenance of organic life, can be attained, it can be reasonably argued that continued treatment is not in the patient's interest (since it can be argued that no truly personal life remains, thus, no personal interests can be promoted. [See 3.2.]

(c) Since persons define their own interests, is there any direct or indirect evidence about how this patient defined interests? If no such evidence exists and if significant medical goals are not being attained, as described in (a), it can be concluded that treatment is not in the patient's interest. [See 2.0–2.1.7.]

(d) If there is evidence, for example, a relative's report or a document, and that evidence shows a preference for treatment (even a treatment which others might consider useless), those preferences should be respected unless heavy costs and burdens are imposed on others.

Thus, relatives may suggest, and physicians accept, certain treatment decisions that meet the above conditions; these decisions could be said to be in the patient's interest and, as such, reflect the ethical principle of respect for the autonomy of the patient.

In our society, frequently no relatives exist or none are interested in a patient's situation. Sometimes, a patient may have several families due to multiple marriages. Close friends or lovers may actually be more concerned than any relatives. In the absence of any legal authority, the physician must not merely select the "next of kin" automatically, but should attempt to discern who, among the interested parties, appears most dedicated to the patient's welfare.

4.2.5 **Ignoring the Patient.** Health professionals sometimes attend to family wishes while neglecting the actual patient.

> EXAMPLE. An elderly woman is brought to a clinic for medical care. The doctor does not acknowledge the presence of the elderly person. He addresses all questions to her daughter. The elderly person does not appear to be mentally incapacitated but sits quietly while her daughter and the doctor converse.

Elderly patients are often treated as if they were incompetent or are infantilized by health professionals. This is a serious failure to respect that patient as a person.

4.2.6 **Relief of Others as a Consideration in Patient Care.** Even when relatives do not express any wishes, the physician may be aware of the burdens imposed on a family or spouse by the impaired life of their relative. Relief of others is often an *important* consideration leading to change in regimen or arrangements for care. Should it ever be *decisive* in deciding not to treat?

> CASE I. A 67-year-old man, who has had a brilliant artistic career, suffers from advanced senile dementia. His devoted family is extremely distressed. His children believe their mother is being precipitated into a breakdown. At present the man is in the hospital with pneumonia. The family halfheartedly tells you to do your best for him. [See 1.4–1.4.4.]

> CASE II. The same as Case I, except there are no children and the husband has been cared for during the last 2 years by his

wife, who herself suffers from severe arthritis and is now exhausted. Since they live in the country, transfer to a nursing home would mean separation.

COMMENT. In Case I, the decision to treat the patient's pneumonia should consider the full range of therapeutic possibilities for this patient (a CARE patient). The goals of restoration of health and maintenance of compromised function can be partially attained. The patient is healthy in all respects except for his somewhat early senility. His life, while of low quality, cannot be considered of minimal quality. The family situation suggests that alternative arrangements for the care of their father can be made and the mother relieved of the burden. In our opinion, the burden on others is not sufficiently weighty to justify a decision not to treat this man's pneumonia.

In Case II, separation of this couple may have serious consequences for both. If both could be domiciled together in a nursing home, the problem would be resolved. If this is impossible, the prospect of separation from her living spouse may be more difficult for this woman than his death. This question should be explored with her. His own irreversible illness offers only a limited achievement of medical goals. The quality of his life is progressively deteriorating. His preferences are not known. In addition, the serious burden that his care imposes on this ill, exhausted, yet devoted wife makes it ethically permissible, with the wife's agreement, not to treat the patient's pneumonia.

Even if ethically permissible (and some will argue it is not permissible at all), the decision in 4.2.6 (II) is troubling. In this case the medical indications, looked at in isolation, call for treatment. The patient's preferences are not known. Quality of life, while poor, is not minimal. A role greater than usual is given to the decision of the spouse. In such a situation, where, despite appearances, the possibility for conflict of interest is great, some external review might be advisable. This could be done informally, by requesting the advice of a disinterested but sympathetic person, such as a clergyman, by requesting Ethics Committee review, or, more formally, by the appointment of a conservator. [See 2.2.9.]

4.2.7 **Organ Transplantation.** The transplantation of tissue from one living person to another involves a medical intervention that puts one person, the donor, at risk (without compensating medical benefit) in order to benefit another, the recipient. This is an unusual situation in medical ethics, which traditionally has not allowed the physician to "do harm" without also benefiting the actual patient. Although some early commentators raised questions about the ethical propriety of being a donor, today this practice is widely considered ethically permissible and praiseworthy. However, it cannot be so easily shown that any person has an ethical *obligation* to donate an organ. Donation should be a free and generous gift. Nevertheless, strong social and psychological pressures may bear on the potential donor. The internist may occasionally be involved as a consultant and adviser to a potential donor.

> CASE. Ms. J. P., a 28-year-old divorced woman, comes to her primary care physician for advice. Her 25-year-old brother, an only sibling, has been found to be in renal failure. He and her parents, as well as the nephrologist, have urged her to be tested for suitability as a donor. She is extremely anxious and says that while she feels guilty, she does not want to be a donor.

COMMENT. It is common in ethics to distinguish between duties and altruism or "acts of supererogation." A person is said to have a duty when another person has a strict right to the performance of some action by the first party. An act of supererogation is done not out of duty but out of generosity; no one has a corresponding right. It is important to maintain this distinction in organ transplantation. The suggestion that an afflicted person has a "right" to the organs of another specific living person has obvious and troubling consequences. In a recent judicial decision, the court implicitly relied upon this ethical distinction in refusing to order a person to "donate" bone marrow to a relative dying of leukemia. Even such a relatively risk-free intervention, with the possibility of significant benefits for the recipient, should be "an act of supererogation."

COUNSEL. The primary care practitioner in the case above is the physician for the woman, not for her brother. "He owes the patient his primary allegiance" (Current Opinions of the Judicial

Council AMA, 1985, Organ Transplantation Guidelines). He may explain to her the risks of being a donor as accurately as possible. He should explore her motivations and fears, as well as the details of her relationship with her family. He might even comment on the desirability, from a medical viewpoint, of the transplantation. He cannot, however, maintain a purely neutral stance since, as her physician, he has an obligation to be her advocate. If she finally decides not to undergo the tests, the physician should support her and be her ally in dealing with family and the specialist. [See 5.4.4.] (EB: ORGAN TRANSPLANTATION.)

4.3   CONFIDENTIALITY

There is a duty incumbent on the physician to maintain in confidence all information learned from or about the patient. This obligation is justified by the right of privacy, by the expectation of the patient, and by the social advantages of the practice of confidentiality. Questions about confidentiality arise when maintaining it might have a harmful effect on another or breaching it might benefit others. In some situations protection of the public is the central issue. In many cases, however, the person who will benefit or be protected by having the information will be a family member. The exceptions to confidentiality for protection of the public are discussed in 4.8. Confidentiality in the family situation is represented by the following cases. (EB: CONFIDENTIALITY, PRIVACY.)

CASE I.   A 46-year-old man is diagnosed as being in imminent danger of a myocardial infarction. He commands the physician not to inform his wife.

CASE II.   A 32-year-old man is diagnosed as suffering from Huntington's chorea. He commands the physician not to inform his wife, whom the physician knows is eager to have children.

CASE III.   A 43-year-old man is treated for gonorrhea 10 days after returning from a business trip. He insists that his wife not be informed.

COMMENT.   In general, the personal assurances of confidentiality (a sort of implicit promise) and the social advantage of maintaining confidentiality require strong justification for any exception. In principle, the *well-founded expectation of serious harm to another specific party* (not others in general) is the most justifiable ethical reason to breach confidentiality. Thus, Case I, in which the wife may benefit by knowing of the husband's illness, does not exemplify a strong justification. His illness does not pose an imminent danger for her. If unusual circumstances existed, for example, the couple was about to depart on a cross-country automobile trip during which he would be the driver, justification for revealing the condition is stronger. The imminent, serious, and likely harm to the wife (from venereal infection) or to future children (from genetic disease) creates stronger justification. Obviously, in any such situation, if the same effect (i.e., protection of another from harm) can be attained without breaching confidentiality, every effort should be made to do so. Such efforts should themselves be ethically proper, avoiding deception and coercion. *Example:* The physician calls the wife of the man in Case III and tells her to come in for a shot, because "something is going around." This stratagem is not only inept but also a deception, which in the long run may cause more harm than it avoids.

> NOTE.   Cases of exceptions to confidentiality are sometimes the most excruciating of ethical dilemmas. The strong obligation to the patient is directly countered by a strong obligation to any other innocent party in danger of serious harm. When a true dilemma is posed, a conscientious decision in either direction is ethically permissible: no consideration is decisive for one over the other.

Other questions arise about confidentiality when protection of the public is an issue. [See 4.8.]

4.4   **COSTS OF CARE**

Costs are incurred whenever medical care is provided. Costs are paid by patients, their families, or by third-party insurers (public or private).

Patients and physicians have always taken costs into account in reaching medical care decisions. Except for emergency treatment, the decisions of persons to seek care and of physicians to accept patients are influenced by financial considerations. In recent years, health care costs have been increasingly assumed by third-party insurers, and both patients and physicians have become less conscious of and less responsible for health costs. Decisions have been based primarily on medical need and/or patient preference, and cost has not been regarded as a relevant consideration. For the last several decades, the medical consensus has been: "Everything that *can* be done and that *might* benefit the patient and that the patient *requests* or at least *does not refuse*—should be done." This attitude is changing rapidly.

New social and political forces designed to constrain health care costs have begun to change the financing of health care and its delivery. Both *regulatory* efforts, such as prospective reimbursement based on diagnosis-related groups (DRGs) and competitive forces such as the rise of proprietary hospital corporations and health maintenance organizations are seen as possible mechanisms for containing health costs.

The critical question facing patients and doctors is how cost containment efforts should influence individual medical decisions. Should patients and physicians factor the legitimate economic interests of third parties—health care institutions, insurance companies, labor unions, corporations, and government—into decisions about appropriate care? Will physicians employed by health care corporations and hospitals be able to balance their professional obligations to patients with their obligations to their employers?

These questions often prompt a polemic response. Some physicians maintain that their only allegiance is to patients and that societal or institutional cost issues are not relevant in reaching decisions about appropriate care for an individual patient. An alternative viewpoint is that physicians have both individual and collective responsibility to use limited societal resources to provide fair and efficient health care to patients. In this latter view, judicious microallocation decisions based upon outcome data are a reasonable approach to providing cost-effective medical care, even if this means that every patient does not receive every diagnostic or therapeutic procedure.

COUNSEL.   It is our view that there are situations—particularly, emergency, ACURE cases [1.3–1.3.3]—that call for radical allegiance to patients and their medical needs irrespective of cost considerations. By contrast, the type and extent of service provided in the other two medical paradigms we have described—CARE [1.4–

1.4.4] and COPE [1.8–1.8.3]—may be affected to a substantial degree by the cost of care, the setting in which care is provided, and by the source of payment for the patient's hospital and physician fees. In 4.4.1 and 4.4.2., we present two situations in which traditional priority of patient need and choice must be retained; in 4.4.3 and 4.4.4., we present situations in which some modification in this traditional approach may be allowed.

.4.1. **Costs to Individuals: Situations in Which Traditional Decision-Making Applies.**   Despite the existence of private and public insurance programs, many individuals still bear a considerable portion of the cost of medical care. In some instances, these costs can be excessive and even ruinous. Individuals may not seek, or may refuse, needed care to avoid these costs.

> CASE.   A 59-year-old man is diagnosed as suffering from acute nonlymphoblastic leukemia. He recently retired, has no health insurance, and has only $20,000 in savings. After discussing his prognosis with his physician, he chooses to spend his life savings on a world cruise with his wife rather than enter chemotherapy. Being a Catholic, he consults his priest, who affirms that his decision is in conformity with the Catholic teaching that medical care, even lifesaving, which in the judgment of the person is too costly can be considered extraordinary and thus not morally obligatory. [See 2.6.1.] The gentleman and his wife enjoy a 3-month tour, 2 months after which he becomes seriously ill and dies at home.

COMMENT.   In this case, the costs of care fall directly upon the patient. He exercises his personal preferences by choosing a world cruise instead of therapy that might prolong his life. His personal preference is sustained by the teaching of his church. The cost of care, in this case, is decisive in the patient's ethical judgment to refuse treatment. In this sense, then, the statement that the cost of care may justify not providing care is certainly acceptable: the patient who bears the burden makes the decision. Even if the physician may consider such a decision foolish or short-sighted, he should respect the decision as an act of the patient's autonomy. [See 2.5.] By contrast, patients who pay for the cost of their medical care from their own savings may request medically appropriate levels of services—such as private rooms, private duty nurses, additional consulting opinions, and expensive diagnostic and therapeutic programs—that might not be offered to patients whose medical costs are supported by third-party insurers.

4.4.2 **Emergency Care.** For economic reasons, some hospitals have refused to accept transfers of medically indigent patients who require services that are available at the hospital. Furthermore, some private hospitals are transferring to public hospitals seriously ill indigent patients who are considered to be "medically stable."

> CASE I. A 26-year-old man was seen in a rural ER, after an automobile accident, with a chief complaint of head trauma and loss of consciousness. Evaluation revealed a transtentorial herniation and an acute subdural hematoma. The patient was treated with dexamethasone, mannitol, and phenytoin. Because the rural hospital was not capable of performing neurosurgery, an attempt was made to transfer the patient to a tertiary care university hospital. When it became clear to the university hospital that the patient lacked medical insurance, the transfer was delayed and the patient ultimately died during transfer to another tertiary facility.

> CASE II. After an automobile accident, a 24-year-old woman who lacked medical insurance was taken to an urban ER and was diagnosed as having sustained a partial transection of the femoral artery in the left thigh. The patient was evaluated by an orthopedic surgeon who felt that the patient's condition was sufficiently stable to permit transfer to a county hospital. The patient's condition worsened during transfer. She underwent surgery to repair the femoral artery but was left with a permanent impairment of the left leg. Several medical experts believed that this permanent damage might have been avoided had the patient been operated on without delay at the first hospital.

COUNSEL. In refusing to accept transfer patients who require emergency care, some hospitals are putting economic considerations ahead of medical indications. Similarly, in transferring patients who require emergency care hospitals are denying patients adequate care and may be increasing their risk.

Such actions are indefensible medically, ethically, and legally. Patients in need of emergency services which a hospital is capable of performing should not be denied admission for economic reasons. Similarly, the only acceptable reason for transferring a "stabilized" medically indigent patient is that the hospital lacks the technical resources to care for the patient's problem. Hospitals must acknowledge their responsibilities to the communities they serve and must provide emergency care within their capabilities to all patients, including the uninsured and medically indigent.

.4.3 **Prospective Payment and Diagnosis-Related Groups.** In October 1983, in an effort to contain medical costs, the Medicare system introduced a form of hospital reimbursement based on uniform payments by Diagnosis Related Groups (DRG). The DRG system has implications for hospitals, physicians, and for hospital–physician relations. The DRG system provides hospitals with incentives to expand "profitable" services (i.e., services they provide efficiently and at a profit), to reduce unprofitable ones, to increase the volume of admissions, to decrease length of stay, and to "skim" cases within a DRG by admitting relatively uncomplicated cases. For physicians, DRGs encourage diagnostic and therapeutic parsimony and mandate efforts to decrease patients' lengths of stay. The impact of these measures on patient outcome remains uncertain, but many physicians feel that these economic pressures may compromise their abilities to provide quality care and may undermine their relationship with patients. Hospital–physician relations may be tested severely by the DRG system, because the institutional goals of efficiency may conflict with physician's judgments about excellent and ethical care.

> EXAMPLE I.   In reviewing its Medicare admissions for 1984–1985, a hospital determines that it earns money from performing cardiac pacemaker replacements (DRG #117) but that it loses money in performing major orthopedic joint procedures (DRG #209). It decides to change its "service mix" by reducing its orthopedic staff and by increasing its cardiology staff.

COMMENT. Hospitals may determine the "service mix" they offer but should do so in a manner consistent with the hospital's resources and mission statement and the needs and resources of their community. Such decisions should be reached collaboratively by the hospital board, the medical staff, and the hospital administration. It is desirable that these decisions be made in consultation with other institutions and community representatives. Whenever possible, such decisions should aim at improving both quality of care and institutional efficiency. Before discontinuing a service, hospitals should determine that equivalent services are available elsewhere in their community.

EXAMPLE II. A 69-year-old, self-employed bricklayer was transferred by helicopter from a rural hospital to a university medical center's ICU comatose, in shock, and with a diagnosis of ARDS, all secondary to Hemophilus pneumonia. After 4 weeks of intensive care, during which time the patient developed multiple complications, including a pseudomonas empyema and cardiac arrest, the patient was weaned successfully from the respirator, transferred from the ICU to a regular hospital room, and eventually recovered and was discharged from the hospital without any permanent end-organ damage. The cost of the patient's stay in the medical ICU was $62,000, far exceeding the Medicare DRG reimbursement. On three occasions while the patient was in the ICU, the attending physician was contacted by the hospital "DRG review committee" and asked to justify the high costs of caring for the patient.

COMMENT. When tensions arise between providing lifesaving patient care (based on medical indications and patient preferences) and cost-effective care (based on economic considerations), these tensions must be resolved in the interest of what is best for the patient and what the patient wants done. Economic considerations are overridden by the patient's critical medical needs. However, as in this case, a regular review of the appropriateness of care is permissible. The costs justify a critical judgment about the nature and extent of benefits to the patient and the curtailment of those that are questionable. Better data on outcomes is still needed in order to validate these determinations.

.4.3 **Health Maintenance Organizations (HMOs).** Health maintenance organizations (HMOs) are a rapidly growing form of prepaid group practice whose membership numbers 15 million patients in 1985 and is expected to increase to 50 million by the 1990s. Because HMOs have a record of containing expenditures, they have attracted considerable support from government and from the insurance industry. Many studies have shown that HMOs decrease cost of care, primarily by decreasing hospital admission rates by 10 to 40%. It remains unclear whether this decreased hospitalization rate results from: (1) self-selected healthier patients who elect to join HMOs; (2) self-selected, cost-conscious physicians who join HMOs and wish to practice a more "conservative" form of medicine; or (3) financial incentives and/ or penalties that encourage HMO physicians to underutilize services—particularly costly in-hospital medical and surgical services of uncertain efficacy.

If cost containment in HMOs is achieved through judicious patient selection or physician self-selection, no ethical dilemmas arise (although interesting public policy questions exist).

Ethical concerns would arise, however, if cost savings were achieved because physicians deliberately restricted services such as diagnostic studies, hospitalization, and surgery in order to increase their share in an end-of-year bonus or in order to conform to preset practice requirements of the HMO.

EXAMPLE. A 52-year-old man with a 3-year history of diabetes and a strong family history of ischemic cardiac disease complains to his HMO physician of 3 weeks of substernal pressure sensation that sometimes occurs at rest. The resting electrocardiogram (EKG) is normal and the patient is referred to a cardiologist at the HMO for further evaluation. The cardiologist orders a multistage exercise test (MSET) but hesitates to include a thallium scintigram as part of the evaluation of atypical chest pain. After a normal MSET, a coronary angiogram reveals two-vessel disease (right coronary 90% occluded, left anterior descending 80% occluded) and the cardiologist decides to treat the patient medically rather than to refer the patient for coronary artery bypass surgery. The HMO to which patient and cardiologist belong is one that distributes a share of the annual profits to physicians if medical care expenditures are kept below a certain level.

COMMENT. The cardiologist-employee described here faces a conflict of interest. Her personal financial benefits are based partly on restricting costly services such as thallium scans and coronary artery bypass graft surgery. On the other hand, her professional responsibilities to the patient require her to provide the patient with the best medical or surgical recommendations, even if these involve a costly surgical procedure. If the patient had three-vessel disease, the cardiologist would have been acting unethically and incompetently in not recommending surgery. Two-vessel coronary disease and the use of thallium scans are, by contrast, both "gray" areas in which considerable technical disagreement remains about appropriate use and wide variation in physician practice exists. In such circumstances, either decision by the HMO cardiologist would be defensible, but one wonders if the conflict of interest noted earlier would not incline the cardiologist toward the less expensive of the alternative treatments.

It is our opinion that patients should be informed about the existence of alternative approaches, but that their physician and plan do not consider these cost-effective. Patients have agreed to this in principle by joining the plan [See 4.4.4.c.]

COUNSEL. Ultimately many of these dilemmas may be resolved by better outcome data. For the present, we must recognize that in unproved "gray" areas, where physician practice patterns differ markedly, HMO physicians are likely to opt for the least costly alternatives. In the absence of outcome data, this position is ethically defensible.

4.4.4   **Use of Cost Considerations in Reaching Clinical Decisions**

In general, then: (a) *Medical indications and patient preferences should retain priority.*   Quality of care should remain a priority and should not be subordinated to cost considerations. Quality of care, however, does not mean all available care. The clinical zeal that urges doing everything for everybody is not good medicine.

In speaking of quality care, we refer not only to care that is diagnostically sound and technically correct. We include care that is rational, that is, no more and no less than is reasonably suited to the problem; cost-effective, that is, known to be the least costly; and ethical, that is, chosen in light of ethical criteria such as we have proposed in this book. Physicians should be trained to apply clinical judgment based on outcome data, technology assessment, and patient preferences to reach decisions.

(b) *Preserve important elements of the doctor–patient relationship.* Newer systems of care, particularly those that divide the physician's allegiance between the patient and the health system, will place enormous stress on the doctor–patient relationship. The most important aspects of the relationship—the physician's special knowledge of the patient and the patient's trust and confidence in the physician—must be preserved. Health services that strive for efficiency should not compromise—indeed, they should strengthen—the bonds between physicians and patients. The physician should serve as the patient's advocate. A physician should advocate for the patient, not all services, but only those needed, those that may benefit the patient, those for which good outcome data exist, and those that the patient wants.

(c) *Maximize patient and physician autonomy within limits imposed by health systems.* While acknowledging the constraints on both patient and physician preferences, we would encourage ways to maximize autonomy and self-determination within an increasingly bureaucratic system. Patients and physicians should exercise autonomy by selecting the kind of health care program in which they wish to participate—for example, prepaid or fee-for-service. If patients are provided sufficient information to make choices, they can express value choices and preferences in selecting a form of health care. Of course, free choice is limited. Constraints are imposed on patients by geography, finances, employment, and medical condition. Similarly, constraints are imposed on physicians by geography, finances, choices of specialty, and the availability of hospital appointments.

Autonomy thus may be expressed by patients primarily in their choosing a system of care at a cost they are willing to pay. Plans differ with respect to coinsurance, deductables, ease of access, selection of physicians and continuity of care with the same physician, range of services, availability of second opinions, and which hospitals a patient will be admitted to when hospitalization is required.

Similarly, physicians express their autonomy by choosing the specialty and system in which they wish to work. In some systems, their diagnostic and treatment options may be limited. The freedom to spend adequate time with patients may be limited. There may be limitations on their hospital privileges. All these may be components of the system that will constrain physician freedom. Still, these restrictions should have been freely accepted when the physician elected to practice in that particular system.

(d) *Provide a local appeals process for patients and also for physicians.* This appeals process should provide a forum where patients' and doctors' complaints and grievances could be addressed. This might involve a clinical care review committee staffed by physicians, nurses, and community representatives. The committee should be charged to ensure that the patient's best medical interests are defended rather than the interests of providers or institutions. The appeals process should also exist in the administration of third-party payors and regulators.

4.5   ALLOCATION OF SCARCE RESOURCES

"Rationing" can have the broad meaning of distributing any limited resource by an allocation mechanism, such as the market. Rationing may have the more specific meaning of allocating some limited resource in terms of a plan that states criteria and priorities. Gasoline and food rationing in war time is an example of this more specific type. Health care in the United States, ranging from primary care to complex technology such as cardiac transplantation, has long been allocated according to implicit rather than explicit criteria.

4.5.1   **Rationing of Medical Care.**   Medical care has always been a scarce resource. The number of physicians, the location of their practice, the ability of persons to pay, the different perceptions of medical need—these factors and many others result in certain allocations of medical care resources. In recent years, however, the question has been raised whether medical resources should be allocated by a plan stating priorities and preferences, and furthermore, whether physicians should be asked to make these allocational choices by balancing societal efficiency against what is best for individual patients. These questions are often asked about expensive, life-saving technologies, such as cardiac and liver transplantation, artificial hearts, and so forth. In general, these are problems of health policy and lie outside the scope of this book.

However, rationing may occasionally become a clinical question. It is a troubling question for physicians who have adhered to the traditional medical ethic of "rendering to each [patient] a full measure of service and devotion" (*AMA Principles of Medical Ethics*). In one sense, no physician renders a "full measure" to any one patient, since physicians have many patients, all of whom must be served. Thus physicians have traditionally rationed their time and efforts. Still, the idea of a plan for rationing medical services is troubling to physicians.

Equally troubling are some of the implicit or explicit criteria suggested as the bases for rationing: age, poverty, lack of insurance senility, "terminal" illness and the need for costly interventions.

EXAMPLE. A 69-year-old businessman with a long history of heart disease and diabetes is admitted to an ICU with fever, hypotension, and shortness of breath. The chest film is consistent with ARDS, and the PO_2 is 50. As the intensive care team prepares to intubate the patient and to insert a Swan–Ganz catheter for hemodynamic monitoring, one resident asks whether this aggressive, costly treatment is appropriate for an elderly man, who has underlying heart disease and diabetes and whose chances of recovering unimpaired from this episode may be no greater than 35 percent.

The resident then distributes a paper written by a noted public official that states:

We've got a duty to die and get out of the way with all our machines and artificial hearts and everything like that, and let our other society, our kids, build a reasonable life. No one who is otherwise healthy should die of a curable disease. On the other hand, no one with a terminal disease should receive endless treatment, if the marginal benefits far exceed the cost. . . .

The economic reality is that every dollar spent on health care is a dollar that we can't spend to retool America, improve our schools or replace our infrastructure. Medical science can make individuals well, but it also can make our nation economically sick.

We are forced to make choices. Do we provide all the extraordinary medical care desperately ill people can take or do we improve our school systems, repair our roads, bridges, dams, and other public facilities?

After reading this paper, several members of the ICU team wonder whether they are doing the right thing by intubating and treating the patient or whether they should begin rationing health care by making tough choices, starting immediately with this 69-year-old man.

COMMENT.   The easiest form of rationing for individual physicians—and the least problematical ethically—involves foregoing medical activities that are useless or unnecessary. Costly, scarce resources should not be expended wastefully on patients who will not benefit. This is an ethical obligation of physicians. Of course, determining when a particular form of intervention is likely to be useless or unnecessary requires acute clinical judgment and is often impossible. Whenever possible, these judgments should be based on medical indications and patient preferences, and less on quality-of-life factors such as age, mental status, or financial resources. The public official quoted is correct when he states: "No one with a terminal disease should receive endless treatment if the marginal benefits far exceed the cost." The problem, as illustrated in the case of the 69-year-old man (who subsequently recovered without any impairment), is that at the time of admission to the hospital, physicians could not be certain whether they were dealing with someone who was "terminally ill" or whether they were dealing with someone who was critically ill but had a significant chance of recovering completely.

4.5.2 **Admission to Programs with Limited Resources.**   Medical care is so organized that certain procedures and therapeutic programs are available only at a few locales or from a few specialists. More persons may need this sort of care than can be accommodated. How should the resources be allocated? All commentators on the ethics of this problem agree that resources should be allocated in a fair manner: What constitutes fairness?

EXAMPLE.   When chronic hemodialysis became available in the late 1960s, the very limited resources required some rationing device. A local committee was established to screen all applicants who had been judged acceptable on medical grounds. The committee was forced to rely on "social worth" criteria, that is, personal and social characteristics that "merited" the treatment. This technique proved unworkable and was much criticized for bias and prejudice.

COMMENT.   Extensive ethical discussion of this issue seems to have reached consensus on the unacceptability of the social worth criteria as a principle of fair distribution. Some commentators have favored "queuing" (first come, first served) although they note that these systems favor the better informed and better connected, who can hurry to the queue. Many favor a lottery, whereby all participate in a drawing of random numbers. This system, however, is faulted because all the pool of needy persons does not exist at any one time. In the most extensive program requiring allocation of scarce resources, the renal transplantation program, selection is now facilitated by the international computerized system for tissue typing. This introduces a major objective consideration, which obviates the biases of social worth and also reduces the uneasiness of having life and death depend purely on "the luck of the draw."

COUNSEL.   The dangers of bias and prejudice inherent in a social worth system advise its rejection as a rationing device. It seems most fair to establish certain very basic objective criteria—for example, medical condition and potential for benefit—and within a pool of those who meet these criteria to select randomly. It may also be useful to establish a "due process" system, which could make exceptions to these criteria. Exceptions should be based on the "Triage" principles.[See 4.5.3.]

4.5.3   **Triage.**   Medical care has long been provided in accord with a plan in one specific situation, battlefield medicine. Since the Napoleonic Wars, military doctors have established priority rules for the treatment of casualties ("triage" is the French word for selection). In recent years, triage rules have been refined and applied to other disasters, such as earthquakes and hurricanes. The rules of triage and its rationale are stated in a handbook of military surgery:

> Priority is to be given to (1) the slightly injured who can be quickly returned to service, (2) the more seriously injured who demand immediate resuscitation or surgery, (3) the "hopelessly wounded" or the dead on arrival. . . . The military surgeon must expend his energies in the treatment of only those whose survival seems likely, in line with the objective of military medicine, which has been defined as "doing the greatest good for the greatest number" in the proper time and place. (*Emergency War Surgery*. Washington, D.C.: Government Printing Office, 1958, pp. 33, 168.)

> EXAMPLE. During World War II, triage decision was made at the policy level to distribute the very limited supply of penicillin first to soldiers with venereal disease rather than to the wounded, since the former could be more quickly returned to battle readiness (and were also infectious).

COMMENT. The citation in a handbook of military surgery, of the Utilitarian Principle [4.0] "the greatest good for the greatest number," makes clear the ethical principle of triage: to return to service those who are needed for the victory, a common good for the army and the nation. Similarly, disaster triage provides priority to persons such as firefighters, public safety officers, and medical personnel so that they can be returned to rescue work. Present disaster and serious danger to the society justify triage rules. This notion is lost in the more casual use of triage, for example, the "triage nurse" in the ER or the application of triage rules to the allocation of ICU beds apart from emergency situations. Lacking the element of present disaster and the destruction of the fabric of social order, rules that subordinate the needs of individuals to the needs of society are not easily justified in medical ethics.

COUNSEL. When treatment or nontreatment decisions must be made on a triage basis, the following conditions should be observed:

(a) There should be an immediate and severe danger to the fabric of society, such that the threat to the society's survival is clear and present.

(b) The selection of certain persons on the basis of their position or skills should be based on the judgment that they will quickly return to their posts.

4.5.4 **Competing Claims to Care.** Situations arise when it can be asked whether the claims of one patient for care override the claims of another. Personnel, time, equipment, beds, and other factors are insufficient to accommodate both. The common-good justification for triage is not present; this is a competition between two rival claimants. In passing, it might be noted that such situations are often avoided by "finding a way" by use of strategems that nurses, in particular, seem particularly ingenious in devising.

> CASE I. Mrs. C. Z., the patient described in 4.1.3, has suffered prolonged anoxia. In this version she is not in persistent vegetative state but has been in deep coma for 7 days. She is sustained on a respirator in the ICU of a small community hospital in a rural area. The victim of an automobile accident is brought to the hospital with a crushed chest, apparent pneumothorax, and broken bones in the extremities. This patient requires a respirator immediately. Mrs. C. Z., of the six patients on the six respirators in the unit, has the poorest prognosis. Should she be removed in favor of the accident victim?

COMMENT. The medical prognosis of Mrs. C. Z. is very dismal. Prolonged anoxia has left her severely damaged. She may soon die or slip into persistent vegetative state, although there is also the unlikely possibility she may emerge from coma. In addition, her death from Hodgkin's disease is certain and probably will occur soon. Her preferences about her care and her life are unknown. Given these considerations, the immediate and serious need of an identifiable other person becomes an important consideration. When that person is in imminent danger of death, and when an effective intervention that will achieve major medical goals [1.1.3] exists the extrinsic factor of scarcity of resources becomes decisive in the decision regarding Mrs. C. Z. It is ethically permissible to remove her from the respirator.

> CASE II. Patient R. A., the drug addict described in 2.8.2, is in need of a second prosthetic heart valve. Several physicians are strongly opposed to providing a second prosthesis. These

physicians offer three reasons: (1) surgery is futile, since the patient will become reinfected; (2) the patient does not care enough about himself to follow a regimen or to abstain from drugs; (3) it is a poor use of societal resources.

COMMENT.   The first and second considerations are discussed in 2.8.2. The third consideration raises new ethical issues. (1) What are the criteria for differentiating good from poor uses of societal resources? Statement of such criteria leads to the problems noted in 3.2.4. (2) There is no guarantee that whatever is "saved" by refusing this patient will be used in any better manner. (3) The resources are, of course, not being "absorbed" by the patient; they are flowing to the hospital, to the physicians and surgeons, to nurses, and so on.

COUNSEL.   The most acceptable ethical justification for refusing to provide a second prosthesis is the medical indication that the risks of surgery and its attendant mortality exceed the risks of managing the patient with medical therapy. Thus, if medically indicated, the surgery should be offered. The ethical obligation to provide surgical assistance is, however, diminished to the extent that the rights of other patients are directly compromised, as explained in *Comment* to Case I.

4.6   RESEARCH VALUES

Many patients are treated under formal research protocols. Care of cancer patients, in particular, may take place within a program for evaluation of chemotherapy. The benefits of research accrue to persons other than the subject of research, namely, to future patients, to the professional doing the research, and to society in general. Even when the subject personally benefits—for example, goes into remission as the result of treatment with an experimental drug—these others are also beneficiaries. Should research values ever be relevant to, important for, or decisive in decisions about care of a particular patient? (EB: HUMAN EXPERIMENTATION, INFORMED CONSENT IN HUMAN RESEARCH.)

4.6.1   **Definition of Clinical Research.**   Clinical research is defined as any clinical maneuver or intervention in accord with a protocol designed to yield generalizable scientific information. (National

Commission for the Protection of Human Subjects of Biomedical and Behavioral Research, The Belmont Report. In Biblio.)

4.6.2   **Regulation of Clinical Research**   Clinical research is governed by guidelines stated in several ethical codes (Nuremburg, Helsinki, American Medical Association). [See Levine, 1981, pp. 259–292]. Regulations promulgated by the DHHS are mandatory for all federally funded research and, in many institutions, for all research. [In Biblio., Federal Register 46.] They require:

(a) Review of proposed research by an institutional review board (IRB) made up of experts—biomedical scientists as well as some "outside" persons. This IRB must evaluate the risks and benefits of the research procedures and certify its approval or disapproval to the funding agency.

(b) Informed consent by any competent participant and permission by guardians for incompetent persons (with special review and protection procedures in specific cases). Many of the ethical problems regarding research must be resolved in the course of IRB review, for example, an appropriate risk/benefit ratio, the details of appropriate disclosure, the suitability of compensation.

4.6.3   **Clinical Research vs. Innovative Treatment.**   It is important to distinguish research from innovative treatment. A physician may choose to employ a drug, approved for other purposes, for a condition in which it has never been used. The clinician may do so primarily as a last resort in the care of a particular patient and without the intention of developing generalizable knowledge, even though the clinician may be able to draw some conclusions in retrospect. This would be "innovative treatment." In research the intent to develop generalizable knowledge is primary and instigates the development of a research plan and the use of methodologies useful in the gathering, analysis, and validation of information. Innovative treatment is not, as such, governed by the codes and regulations that govern research. However, it should be governed by the same spirit. The advice of knowledgeable colleagues should be sought, a risk/benefit ratio as accurate as possible should be worked out, and the consent of the patient to be the subject of a yet untried treatment should be obtained. In addition, innovative treatment should be designed as much as possible like research, so that the social benefit of valid knowledge can be obtained. Finally, in doubtful cases, clinicians should seek the advice of the IRB about the advisability of innovative treatment.

4.6.4 **Ethical Problems in Clinical Research.**   All clinician-researchers should honor the ethics of clinical research by abiding by the requirements of informed consent of subjects and review of protocols by competent bodies. However, in clinical situations ethical problems may still arise. It might be asked whether a particular patient, who is in general an appropriate candidate for an approved protocol, should be approached because the risk/benefit equation is questionable in this patient's case.

This problem might arise in situations in which a new drug, believed to be of potential benefit from preliminary animal and human investigations, is to be compared in a formal clinical trial against a placebo.

> EXAMPLE I.   When the polio vaccine first became available, it was tested in large surveys against a placebo. Many clinicians believed in the efficacy of the vaccine and were concerned that some preventable poliomyelitis—including paralysis and death—would occur in the control subjects who did not receive the actual vaccine.

COMMENT.   Randomized clinical trials are a relatively recent development. They are essential to the development of effective and safe therapies. In double-blind trials, neither the doctor nor the patient knows whether the patient is receiving a drug or a placebo. Some physicians find this situation clinically and ethically unacceptable. Some physicians are concerned that their patients may be randomized to an inferior therapy. However, a properly designed controlled trial would be one in which a true null hypothesis exists so that neither of the proposed therapies could be regarded as definitely better than the other. Also, prejudice about efficacy can cause serious harm. Early neonatology provides a tragic example. When administration of high dosages of oxygen was suspected as the course of retrolental fibroplasia, a randomized trial was resisted because of the conviction, unconfirmed by evidence, that high dosage was necessary for effective therapy. As a result of this resistance, many more babies suffered eye damage than would have otherwise. It can be asked whether patients should be continued on protocol, or new patients entered, when a clinician-researcher believes the majority of patients whom he has treated seem to benefit from one experimental drug rather than the standard treatment.

> EXAMPLE II. A clinician is entering patients in a randomized, double-blind trial of a drug to prevent angina. He suspects from the side effects which drug is the standard one and which the experimental. He also has the impression that patients on the suspected research drug are doing much better.

COMMENT. The investigator seems caught between two obligations, the duty to benefit the patient and the contractual duty to carry out the trial (and the more abstract duty to advance medical science). In principle, the duty to benefit the patient supersedes all others. However, in this situation, suspicion and clinical impressions do not override the scientifically founded uncertainty about where benefit lies. That uncertainty will be resolved only when properly collected data are analyzed. Only if the individual clinical investigator is convinced, and if the use or nonuse of a certain drug may cause harm, does it become unethical to proceed. Soundly designed clinical trials should have oversight mechanisms to monitor trends, to deal with the problems of clinical impressions, and to terminate the trial should the evidence of distinct benefit or harm become persuasive.

4.7   **TEACHING VALUES**

Many patients receive care in institutions where clinical teaching is done. Their disease and its diagnosis and treatment provide an opportunity for students in the health sciences to learn the skills necessary for their profession. Often, actual treatment will be provided by a student. It is possible that some clinical decisions are made with a view to these teaching values and that such decisions may conflict with the patient's interests and/or wishes. (EB: MEDICAL EDUCATION.)

> CASE I. A 52-year-old obese woman requires a lumbar puncture. The procedure is supervised by a second-year resident attended by four medical students. It is performed on a shaky bed in a four-bed ward without draping. The resident leaves the room after giving instructions to the students and watching one of them make several unsuccessful attempts to insert the needle

in the spinal canal. "You've got to start somewhere," the resident remarks.

COMMENT. There is no ethical *problem* in this case; it is an ethical outrage. No consideration is shown to the patient's feelings, supervision is inadequate, easily arranged accommodations are not made. Students are often offended by being placed in such situations. As low persons in the medical school hierarchy, students may feel an ethical conflict and not know how, or to whom, to express their feelings.

Although the case described is an ethical insult rather than an ethical problem, we must be aware that relatively inexperienced students perform many procedures in teaching hospitals, including blood drawing, intravenous insertions, lumbar punctures, paracenteses, thoracenteses, and occasional endotracheal intubations. Students often remark (in private) about their feelings concerning these procedures. They are eager to learn these skills and believe they must master these techniques in order to function effectively as physicians. Still, they are not sure how to approach the patient and how much disclosure is appropriate for the patient's informed consent, particularly for relatively innocuous, albeit discomforting, procedures, such as venipuncture.

CASE II. A 74-year-old man with chronic obstructive pulmonary disease is admitted in mild respiratory failure and with diffuse bronchospasm. His respiratory condition probably does not require insertion of a Swan–Ganz catheter for hemodynamic monitoring. Nevertheless, the chief resident suggests a catheter be placed; one of her reasons for this choice is to allow an inexperienced intern to practice this technical procedure.

COMMENT. Procedures involving any risk should be performed only for valid diagnostic or therapeutic purposes. Risky procedures should not be done exclusively or even partially for their teaching value. Thus, in Case II, the intern's need for additional practice should not affect the chief resident's clinical judgment. If the procedure is harmless, such as palpation or auscultation, or involves only minor inconvenience, such as asking a patient with ataxic gait to get up from a chair and walk across the room, or minor discomfort, as extension and flexion of an arthritic limb, patients may be requested to allow the procedure. Harmless procedures may also be done on patients who are mentally incapacitated.

4.7.1 **Consent to Be a Teaching Subject.** Persons who enter teaching hospitals usually sign a general consent to that effect. Many patients, particularly those who are seriously ill at the time of admission or for other reasons are unable to comprehend the meaning of the teaching hospital consent form, have probably not given adequate informed consent to be used as teaching subjects. They should be asked specifically about each episode of teaching. The demonstration procedure should be explained to the patient; the fact that the procedure will be done by a student and that it is for teaching rather than for their care (or in addition to the care) should be made clear. The request should be made politely and a refusal accepted graciously. Patients are amazingly generous in consenting to participate in the education of medical students in teaching hospitals. Many patients provide their histories to, and allow examination by, five or more students without complaint. In the light of these observations, it is particularly important that, when the occasional patient refuses to participate in one or another teaching exercise, the student and the faculty respect that patient's wishes absolutely and not threaten or intimidate the patient in any way. Medical students and physicians must remember that *individual* patients are not obligated to participate in the training of society's future physicians. They almost invariably are eager to do so, and physicians should acknowledge their enormous debt to patients for the patients' unquestioning generosity.

Many patients enjoy being asked to be teaching subjects. Medical students often pay them more attention than their regular physicians, particularly in teaching settings. This is a benefit for the patient. However, it should not of itself be presumed as the justification for using patients for teaching purposes.

4.8 **PUBLIC SAFETY AND WELFARE**

Physicians have responsibilities to protect and promote the public health. These may, on occasion, appear to jeopardize the welfare of particular patients or to impose particular burdens on them.

Quarantine of carriers of infection is a decision for the benefit of persons other than the patient: The patient's liberty is restricted in an effort to protect the public. This is also the case with mandatory immunization. Similarly, the reporting of infectious diseases to the health department is required by law in most jurisdictions. This also is intended to warn and to provide preventive or therapeutic measures to persons other than the patient. Finally, dangers of other sorts, such as the violent threats of a patient to do bodily harm to others, may recommend forms of treatment, from involuntary detention to use of tranquilizing or antipsychotic drugs. What are the conditions that justify any treatment decision which appears to be more beneficial for others than for the patient? Is it ever justified to make a decision clearly not for the patient's benefit but for the well-being of others? (EB:PUBLIC HEALTH, SOCIAL MEDICINE.)

CASE I.   The student in 1.3 has meningococcal rather than pneumococcal meningitis. He refuses therapy and wishes to return to the dorm.

CASE II.   A 28-year-old man who has been under your care for severe peptic ulcer impresses you as somewhat bizarre in attitude and behavior. You suspect that he suffers from a psychotic disorder and ask him whether he is seeing a psychiatrist. He calmly responds that he was once under treatment for schizophrenia but has been well for years. Then, in the course of an office visit, he casually tells you he would like to see the mayor dead and was thinking of assassinating him. Should you report your patient to the police?

CASE III.   A 27-year-old nurse in a dialysis unit is hepatitis B antigen-positive. She is reluctant to inform her social contacts and resists any restriction of her professional activities. She approaches a private practitioner for advice. Should the practitioner take steps to ensure that her social contacts are informed of her condition? Should the practitioner take steps to see that her professional activities are restricted?

CASE IV.   A school board considers a policy of requiring HTLV-III antibody test for all teachers in order to prevent the spread of Acquired Immune Deficiency Syndrome (AIDS).

COMMENT. In Case I, meningococcal meningitis is an infectious disease. Infectivity is high and thus the return of the student to the dormitory puts fellow students at high risk of a serious disease. Protection of specific others from a serious harm justifies the decision to detain the student and to treat. In Case II the danger to others is less clear. This patient is obviously in need of psychiatric treatment and should be persuaded to seek it. The threat, as is often the case, may be empty. Several of the conditions that would justify breach of confidentiality are present: An identifiable person is threatened, and serious harm could be done. The condition that is absent is assurance that the patient is really likely to take action. The consequences to the patient of being reported to the police might be significant. The consequences of reporting "suspicious persons" on the basis of suspicions aroused in medical care encounters might also be socially undesirable since it might inhibit persons in need of help from seeking it.

In Case III, the infectivity of the nurse is low; the possibilities for contact are extensive and difficult to limit. She is capable of arranging her social contacts so as to avoid infecting others. In terms of her personal life and social behavior, the matter should be left to her own responsibility. In terms of her professional life, she has a direct obligation to protect her patients from harm. If she refuses to do this by reporting herself and by restricting her activities voluntarily, the physician has a duty to report her. In Case IV, the information gained from HTLV-III antibody tests in a population without risk factors for AIDS yields a high number of false positives, and the implications of antibody positivity for actual disease or infectivity are uncertain. At the same time, possibility of harm to the reputation, employment, and insurability of individuals is serious. Thus, the proposed policy to test all teachers is reprehensible.

COUNSEL. The ethical obligation to protect others, even at the expense of interfering with the patient's liberty and privacy, is strongest in Case I: There is a genuine threat of serious harm to particular, identifiable persons. In Case II we do not consider the likelihood of harm sufficiently great to justify a breach of confidentiality, although added circumstances may heighten assurance that the patient is likely to act out his fantasies. In Case III, the more remote risk, the responsibility of the person for her own behavior and the practical impossibility of protecting everyone with whom she deals do not add up to an obligation to protect others, except the patient population with whom this person deals as a health professional. In Case IV, health professionals should not cooperate with school board policy.

4.8.1   **Legal Implications.**   Most jurisdictions have statutes requiring the physician to report cases of certain sorts, such as venereal disease, gunshot and knife wounds, and child abuse. These statutes should be obeyed when the physician has practical certainty that the reportable fact is present. Exceptions should not be lightly made. (Many physicians fail to report child abuse or venereal disease, particularly when the parents or patients are "respectable"; this failure is reprehensible.) In some localities, reporting practices have fallen into disuse or follow-up procedures by health departments are casual. Where a report would be useless, the obligation of confidentiality rules. Most jurisdictions also have statutes allowing physicians to detain mentally disturbed persons and to treat them when such persons are dangerous to themselves or others. These statutes usually set out specific conditions and limits. Physicians should acquaint themselves with the precise provisions of these statutes in the jurisdictions where they practice. [See 2.7.3.]

In one precedent-setting case, *Tarasoff v. Regents* (1976), a student informed his psychotherapist that he intended to kill a young woman. This was not communicated to the woman, who was subsequently murdered. The California Supreme Court ruled that the psychiatrist and the psychologist had a positive duty to take reasonable steps to protect third parties from harm. The serious danger of violence to an identifiable person was a consideration that, in the opinion of the court, overrode the obligation to preserve confidential information obtained in the course of psychiatric therapy. In the court's opinion, existence of such a duty would not deter persons from seeking help from psychotherapists. It is unclear how this decision would apply to other practitioners who obtain similar information in the course of providing general care. They should seek consultation from persons expert both in mental health and in the law. Every effort should be made to obtain psychiatric help for the patient. If the physician judges the threat to be real and likely to be carried out, the matter should be reported to authorities. (EB: CONFIDENTIALITY.)

4.8.2 **Conflict of Interest for the Physician.** The occupational physician, the military physician, and the prison or police physician may encounter conflicts of interest. As physicians they are obliged to serve those who come to them as patients; as employees they have obligations to their employers. Ethical problems may arise, particularly about confidentiality and disclosure.

> CASE I.   The dialysis nurse described in 4.8 is examined by the hospital's Employee Health Service physician. This examination is required by hospital regulations. When the physician tells the nurse she is hepatitis B antigen-positive, she insists he not report her to the director of the dialysis unit.

COMMENT.   The physician in this case has accepted responsibilities to the institution as well as responsibilities to particular patients. This dual relationship should be clear to the patient in this situation. The physician should report this patient. The dual relationship may not be clear in many situations where workers approach company physicians. It is imperative that the dual relationship be made clear whenever it is relevant and that its implications be spelled out for the patient-employee.

> CASE II.   A worker in an industry using kepone visits the company physician about a persistent cough. The physician does a cursory physical and prescribes a cough medicine. It is company policy not to investigate symptoms of this sort too aggressively until they become demonstrably more serious. It is also policy not to suggest to worker-patients the potential for lung disease or to make employee health records available to them.

COMMENT.   The company policy is manifestly unethical since it causes persons to be deprived of the possible benefits of early diagnosis and treatment. The physician who accepts such a policy clearly acts unethically, since duties to patients are disregarded without the patient's being made aware of the physician's dual role. The Code of Ethics of the American Society for Occupational Medicine requires physicians working in such settings to "avoid allowing other medical judgment to be influenced by any conflict of interest" and "to accord highest priority to the health and safety of the individual in the workplace" (J Occup Med, 1976, 8). This implies that conflicts should be resolved in favor of individual patients, even if this is to the detriment of the company and the physician. Physicians accepting positions with dual responsibilities should be certain that their employers will allow them to abide by the ethical code.

4.8.3 **Torture and Punishment by Physicians.** It should go without saying that physicians employed in prisons and by police should not participate in interrrogation and punishment of suspects and convicts. Under no circumstances should they participate in torture. They should not participate in civil executions, except to declare death, which they alone can do under the law in most jurisdictions. In these activities there is no patient benefit. (EB: PRISONERS.)

4.8.4 **Strikes by Physicians.** In recent years physicians have organized to withhold medical services for a period of time in order to win concessions for themselves or for patients.

> EXAMPLES. All anaesthesiologists in a particular state agree not to assist at any elective surgery in order to protest excessive malpractice insurance premiums; the house officers of a city hospital refuse to provide anything but emergency care in order to protest the inadequate facilities, working conditions, and staffing of the institution.

The form of withholding services is crucial. Thus, reasons of self-interest are much less weighty than reasons of correcting genuine deficiencies in patient care. Withholding only services not urgently needed is more justifiable than withholding all services (a distinction that may be difficult in practice). Nevertheless, the fact that the withholding of service penalizes particularly vulnerable persons, namely, patients and potential patients, makes concerted withholding of services ethically dubious even when justifications are strong. Physicians, as a group, have considerable social authority and political influence in our society; they have many means of redressing inequities short of withholding their services from those who need them.

4.9   **PERSONAL AND SOCIAL RESPONSIBILITIES**

Physicians, like all persons, have to allocate their time, attend to personal and family affairs, and earn an income. They work within certain administrative structures and within certain relationships with peers. They are affected by public policies, such as the institution of federal programs like Medicare or the rates of reimbursement for certain procedures. In addition, their habitual or occasional emotional and psychological states influence their decisions. While it is not possible here to analyze these factors, their presence and influence on decision making should be noted and, in particular situations, carefully scrutinized.

Physicians also have social responsibilities as citizens. Some of these responsibilities arise from the knowledge and skills proper to the medical profession and from the expectations the public has about the profession's function in society. Physicians, as individuals and as organized groups, should take positions on activities and policies that have implications for the health of the society. Traditionally the profession exercised leadership in efforts to protect communities from quackery, from communicable disease, and from contaminated food and water. Today professional leadership should be exerted in such areas as health education about personal behavior; the use of tobacco, alcohol, and drugs; housing and nutrition; environmental pollution; highway safety; occupational safety; and domestic and military nuclear policy. Physicians also exercise considerable authority over the ways in which medical care is organized. The profession bears a corporate responsibility to ensure that the provision of care is not dominated by self-interest but by the health needs of the public. Finally, the profession continues to enjoy broad autonomy in determining standards of care and over the admission, education, and discipline of physicians. It thus bears the responsibility for maintaining high standards, effective programs of physician education at every level, and a fair but efficacious disciplinary system for the protection of the public. (EB: SOCIAL MEDICINE; POVERTY AND HEALTH; PUBLIC HEALTH; WARFARE; RACISM AND HEALTH; ALCOHOL, USE OF; DRUG USE; ENVIRONMENTAL ETHICS; FOOD POLICY; POPULATION ETHICS.)

BIBLIOGRAPHY

4.0–4.2 *Socioeconomic Factors*

Bayer, R., Caplan, A., Daniels, N. *In Search of Equity, Health Needs and the Health Care System*. New York: Plenum, 1983.

Caplan, A. Ethical and policy issues in the procurement of cadaver organs for transplantation. N Engl J Med, 1984, 311:981.

Daniels, N. *Justice and Health Care Delivery*. Cambridge, England: University Press, 1985.

Doudera, E., Cranford, R. *Institutional Ethics Committees and Health*

Care Decision Making. Ann Arbor, Mich.: Health Administration, Inc., 1984.

Ethics Committee Newsletter. Boston, American Society of Law and Medicine (765 Commonwealth Ave.).

Fost, N., Cranford, R. Hospital ethics committees. JAMA, 1985, 253:2687.

Katz, J., Capron, A. *Catastrophic Diseases: Who Decides What?* New York: Russell Sage Foundation, 1975.

President's Commission for the Study of Ethical Problems in Medicine and Biomedical and Behavioral Research. *Deciding to Forego Life-Sustaining Treatment*. (See General References.)

President's Commission for the Study of Ethical Problems in Medicine and Biomedical and Behavioral Research. *Securing Access to Health Care*. (See General References.)

Purtillo, R. Ethics consultation in the hospital. N Engl J Med, 1984, 311:983.

Rosner, F. Hospital medical ethics committees. A review of their development. JAMA, 1985, 253:2693.

Shelp, E. E. (ed.) *Justice and Health Care*. Boston, Dordrecht, and London: D. Reidel, 1981.

Sherlock, R., Dingus, M. Families and the gravely ill: Roles, rules and rights. J Am Geriat Soc, 1985, 33:121.

4.3 *Confidentiality*

Cooper, A. Duty to warn third parties. JAMA, 1982, 248:431.

Meyers, D. *Medicolegal Implications*, Chapter 17. (See General References.)

Miller, R., Schaffer, K., Meisel, A. Ethical and legal issues related to the use of computer programs in clinical medicine. Ann Intern Med, 1985, 102:529.

Osterholm, M., Bowman, R., Chopek, M., et al. Screening donated blood and plasma for HTLV antibody. N Engl J Med, 1985, 312:1185.

Perkins, H., Jonsen, A. Conflicting duties to patients: The sexually active hepatitis B carrier. Ann Intern Med, 1981, 94:523.

Siegler, M. Confidentiality in medicine: A decrepit concept. N. Engl J Med, 1982, 307:1518.

Weiss, B. Confidentiality expectation of patients, physicians and medical students. JAMA, 1982, 247:2695.

Ziporyn, T. Hippocrates meets the data banks: Patient privacy in computer age. JAMA, 1984, 252:317.

4.4 *Costs of Care*

Avorn, J. Benefit and cost analysis in geriatric care: Turning age discrimination into health policy. N Engl J Med, 1984, 310:1294.

Bayer, R., Callahan, D., Fletcher, J., et al. The care of the terminally ill: Morality and economics. N Engl J Med, 1983, 309:1490.

Curran, W. Economic and legal considerations in emergency care. N Engl J Med, 1985, 312:374.

Detsky, A., Stricker, S., Mulley, A., Thibault, G., et al. Prognosis, survival and the expenditure of hospital resources for patients in the intensive care unit. N Engl J Med, 1981, 305:667.

Johnson, D. Death and the dollar sign: Medical ethics and cost containment. JAMA, 1984, 252:223.

McPhee, S., Myers, L., Lo, B. Cost containment confronts the physician. Ann Intern Med, 1984, 100:604.

Siegler, M. The progression of medicine: From physician paternalism to patient autonomy to bureaucratic parsimony. Arch Intern Med, 1985, 145:713.

Stone, A. Law's influence on medicine and medical ethics. N Engl J Med, 1985, 312:309.

4.5 *Allocation of Scarce Health Resources*

Almeder, R. Scarcity and basic medical care. In Biomedical Ethics Review. J. M. Humber, R. F. Almeder (eds). Clifton, N.J.: Humana Press, 1983.

Eisenberg, J. The internist as gatekeeper: Preparing the general internist for a new role. Ann Intern Med, 1985, 102:537.

Engelhardt, H.T. Allocating scarce medical resources and the availability of organ transplantation—some moral presuppositions. N Engl J Med, 1984, 311:66.

Evans, R. Health care technology and the inevitability of resource allocation and rationing decisions. JAMA, 1983, 249:2047, 2208.

Fuchs, V. The rationing of medical care. N Engl J Med, 1984, 311:1572.

Iglehart, J. Medical care for the poor: A growing problem. N Engl J Med., 1985, 313:59.

Leaf, A. The doctor's dilemma and society's too. N Engl J Med, 1984, 310:718.

Levine, R. Total artificial heart implantation—eligibility criteria. JAMA, 1984, 252:1458.

Menzel, P. *Medical Costs, Moral Choices*. New Haven, Conn.: Yale University Press, 1983.

President's Commission for the Study of Ethical Problems in Medicine and Biomedical and Behavioral Research. *Securing Access to Health Care*. (See General References.)

Relman, A. The new medical–industrial complex. N Engl J Med, 1980, 303:963.

Schwartz, W., Aaron, H. Rationing health care: Lessons from Great Britain. N Engl J Med, 1984, 310:52.

Siegler, J. Should age be a criterion in health care? Hastings Cent Rep, 1984, 14:24.

Singer, D., Carr, P., Mulley, A., Thibault, G., et al. Rationing intensive care—physician response to a resource shortage. N Engl J Med, 1983, 309:1155.

Wooley, R. Ethical issues in the implantation of the total artificial heart. N Engl J Med, 1984, 310:292.

4.6 Research Values

The Belmont Report: Ethical Principles in Research with Human Subjects. National Commission for Protection of Human Subjects of Biomedical and Behavioral Research, 1978.

Blumberg, B., Fox, R., The Daedalus effect: Changes in ethical questions relating to hepatitis B virus. Ann Intern Med, 1985, 102:390.

Cassileth, B., Miller, D. Attitudes toward clinical trials among patients and the public. JAMA, 1982, 248:968.

IRB: A Review of Human Subjects Research. Hastings-on-Hudson, N.Y. Institute for Society, Ethics and the Life Sciences. (Published 10 times yearly.)

Levine, R. Ethics and Regulation of Clinical Research. Baltimore, Md. Urban and Schwarzenberg, 1981.

Levine, R. Informed consent in research and practice. Arch Intern Med, 1983, 143:1229.

Lipsett, M. On the nature and ethics of phase I clinical trials of cancer chemotherapy. JAMA, 1982, 248:941.

Protection of human subjects of biomedical and behavioral research. Code of Federal Regulations Title 5. Public Welfare Part 46. Federal Register 46(16) January 26, 1981.

Schafer, A. The ethics of randomized clinical trials. N Engl J Med, 1982, 307:719.

Silverman, W. Human Experimentation. Oxford: Oxford University Press, 1985.

Taylor, K., Margolese, R., Soskolne, C. Physician's reasons for not entering eligible patients in a randomized clinical trial for breast cancer. N Engl J Med, 1984, 310:1364.

Weintraub, M. Ethical concerns and guidelines in research in geriatric pharmacology and therapeutics: Individualization, not codification. J Am Geriat Soc, 1984, 32:44.

4.8 Public Safety and Welfare

Cassell, C., Jameton, A. Medical Responsibility and Thermonuclear War. Ann Intern Med 1982, 97:426.

Code of ethical conduct for physicians providing occupational health services. Journal of Occupation Med, 1976, 8:cover.

Conte, J., Hadley, W., Sande, M., et al. Infection control guidelines for patients with acquired immune deficiency syndrome. N Engl J Med, 1983, 309:740.

Curran, W. The ethics of medical participation in capital punishment. N Engl J. Med, 1980, 302:226.

Daniels, N. On the picket line: Are doctor's strikes ethical? Hastings Cent Rep, 1978, 8(1):24.

Himmelstein, J., Frumkin, H. The right to know about toxic exposures: Implications for physicians. N Engl J Med, 1985, 312:687.

Jonsen, A., Jameton, A. The Social Responsibilities of Physicians. J Philos Med, 1977, 2:376.

Sagan, L., Jonsen, A. Medical ethics and torture. N Engl J Med, 1976, 294:1427.

5

PEDIATRIC ETHICS

5.0 Chapters 1 through 4 outline the basic considerations and issues in ethical decisions about patients. In all cases, the patients have been adults—persons who have reached an age at which they are presumed, legally and ethically, to have the capacity to express preferences and make decisions. We now turn to ethical questions arising in the care of infants and children. In general, the same basic considerations laid out in the previous chapters apply to pediatrics, namely, medical indications, preferences, quality of life, socioeconomic factors. However, each of these differ in significant ways. This chapter will highlight those differences. The reader of this chapter must recall that the brief treatment found here is based upon the broader discussions in the previous chapters; only very special conditions about pediatric care call for extended mention. Commentary is also required to interpret the so-called ''Baby Doe Regulations'' (Federal Regulations: Child Abuse and Neglect Prevention and Treatment). Ethical issues in obstetrics and reproductive medicine are not included in this chapter. Even though many of these issues shade into pediatrics, they require a more extended analysis than can be provided here.

NOTE: The numbering system directs the reader back to the relevant sections in the previous chapters: 5 is the number of this chapter; 1, 2, 3, and 4 refer to the previous chapters of that number. Thus, all 5.1 numbers refer the reader back to the general considerations in Chapter One, Medical Indications. The third numbers designate the sequence of paragraphs in this chapter; then, if useful, a direct reference to the section in the previous chapter will be given; thus, 5.1.4 (1.6) designates the fourth paragraph of the present chapter's discussion of Orders Not to Resuscitate; Section 1.6 in Chapter 1 contains the fuller exposition of that topic.

5.1   **MEDICAL INDICATIONS**

In discussing an ethical problem arising in pediatrics, the same pattern should be used as for adult patients. First, review the indications for diagnostic and therapeutic procedures based on the evaluation of the patient's physical condition. From the viewpoint of ethics, these indications consist not only of certain physical findings and available techniques, but also a judgment about the nature of the physician's responsibility and the goals of medical intervention.

5.1.1   **The Responsibilities of the Pediatrician and the Goals of Pediatrics.**   In general, the responsibilities of the pediatrician are the same as those for all physicians: to benefit the patient and to refrain from harm. The goals of medical intervention are the same, whether the patient is adult or infant: restoration of health, relief of symptoms, restoration of impaired function, saving and prolonging endangered life.

However, the pediatrician's exercise of these responsibilities has some special features:

(a) The patient is very often too immature to formulate preferences or make judgments about personal interests and well being. As the patient matures, uncertainty about the relevance of preferences to treatment decisions may arise, as they may conflict with preferences of adults.

(b) The patient is usually under the care of adult parents or guardians whose authority is extensive, but not absolute, and whose legal role may be unclear.

(c) The patient may have siblings for whose well-being the parents are equally responsible.

(d) The patient is at the beginning of life and prediction of its adult values, preferences, and qualities is difficult, if not impossible.

(e) Children constitute the population of the future; thus, medical care decisions and health policy about them have an impact far beyond the present.

These features of pediatric medicine will modify the exercise of the basic responsibilities that pediatricians share with all physicians. In particular, the duty to respect the choices of an autonomous person differs significantly when that person with whom the pediatrician communicates is a parent or guardian and not the patient, who is here considered incapable of autonomous choice.

5.1.2   **Forms of Disease.**   The three forms described at 1.2 are generally relevant to pediatrics. However, one of the common ethical problems is caused by the conjunction of two of these forms: the presence of a potentially curable or manageable disorder (ACURE, CARE) in a child known to have a constitutional disorder involving limited mental development (COPE).

> EXAMPLES: A newborn is noted to have the stigmata of Down's Syndrome and to have a correctable intestinal anomaly such as duodenal atresia or esophogeal fistula; a 12-year-old boy with Down's Syndrome has a congenital heart condition that, unless surgically corrected, will reduce life expectancy.

The problem posed by this conjunction will be discussed under 5.3.

5.3 (1.5)   **Decisions to Terminate or Withhold Intervention as Medically Inefficacious or Futile.**   Interventions are inefficacious when a competent practitioner judges that it will not effect the medical goal to which it is directed; it is futile if it might do so, but only in so fleeting or temporary a fashion that the condition will return or other medical conditions will supervene to obliterate the benefit.

In the above examples, surgery will certainly attain the goal of correcting the atresia or fistula; it will probably produce normal longevity for the twelve-year-old. From the viewpoint of medical indications, surgery is appropriate in both cases. The relevance of quality of life considerations is discussed in 5.3. However, in other cases, medical intervention may be considered as inefficacious or futile.

CASE I.   An anacephalic infant is born to a mother who had no prenatal care. Large portions of the cranium are absent and the forebrain and much of the brain stem is missing. However, the infant is gasping at birth.

CASE II.   A fetus is delivered by spontaneous abortion at 23 weeks gestation, weighing 360 gms and is asphyxiated at birth.

CASE III.   A 4-year-old child, absent from home for about 2 hours, is found at the bottom of a nearby icy pond. Full resuscitative efforts restore heartbeat and respiration, but after 6 weeks with ventilatory support, there is no evidence of spontaneous breathing, although electroencephalography indicates cerebral activity. The child develops bacterial pneumonia.

COMMENT.   Reasonable clinical judgments of futility or inefficacy are a sound justification for a decision not to intervene or to discontinue medical interventions. This ethical justification is acknowledged in the Federal Regulations, "Child Abuse and Neglect Prevention and Treatment Program" (45 CFR 1340), which direct state child protective agencies to ensure that infants are not deprived of medically indicated treatment for life-threatening conditions. These regulations state that treatment is not required, "when the provision of such treatment would merely prolong dying, not be effective in ameliorating or correcting all of the infant's life-threatening conditions, or otherwise be futile in terms of the survival of the infant." [At 14888.]

COUNSEL.   In all the above cases, it is reasonable to judge that interventions to sustain organic functions will be incapable of restoring these functions to independent activity. It is ethically correct to withhold or withdraw interventions.

CASE IV.   An infant born at 32 weeks gestation and weighing 1,100 gms., is resuscitated at birth and develops severe hyaline membrane disease. During the next 12 weeks the infant suffers a grade IV intraventricular hemorrhage, chronic lung disease requiring continuous mechanical ventilation, and undergoes surgery for removal of all but 20 cm of necrotic terminal ilium.

There is no sign of clinical improvement. The infant now develops candida sepsis.

CASE V.   A 7-year-old girl with acute myelogenous leukemia, suffers a second relapse. Her previous courses of chemotherapy were associated with severe toxic effects. She is extremely fearful of a return to the hospital.

COMMENT and COUNSEL.   Cases IV and V illustrate the category of futility: it is remotely possible that continuing therapy may effect a change for the better but experience suggests that its continuance will bring only brief time and more suffering. All honest and serious efforts at treatment have been exhausted. It is ethically permissible to discontinue treatment.

CASE VI.   An infant is born with hypoplastic left ventricle, confirmed by cardiac ultrasound. Informed of the lethal nature of this defect, the parents ask whether there is any reasonable hope of saving their child's life.

COMMENT and COUNSEL.   Attempts have been made to correct this fatal condition by a surgical procedure of uncertain efficacy and by transplantation of an animal heart. Both procedures are clearly experimental; indeed, the second currently may lack the scientific basis required for sound clinical research. It is reasonable to judge that such rescue efforts fall into the category of the inefficacious or futile, although, given the proper conditions for research on children (5.4.5), they might be ethically undertaken.

4 (1.6)   **Orders Not to Resuscitate.**   In general, the conditions for an order not to initiate cardiopulmonary resuscitation are the same for a child as for an adult, with the exception of the patient's consent. However, resuscitation of the asphyxiated newborn raises special questions.

CASE I.   Same as Case II above.

CASE II.   An infant, born at 33 weeks gestation, appears to be microcephalic, with low-set, posteriorly stated ears. A single umbilical artery is noted, in addition to an oddly shaped chest. The birth had been precipitous, the mother having received Demerol IM 1 hour preceding. Apgar score is 1 at 1 minute; heart rate 100 beats/min.

In Case I, it is ethically correct to decide before birth or at birth, not to resuscitate. Experience indicates that even if resuscitated, this very small premature infant will not survive. In Case II, resuscitation should be attempted, since the nature of the child's congenital problems is not clear. The fact of resuscitation does not prohibit a later decision to withdraw treatment, based either on medical indications or on the considerations discussed in 5.3. For a discussion of the absence of any ethical difference between not initiating and terminating an intervention, see 3.2 COMMENT.

5.1.5 (1.7)   **Brain Death and Persistent Vegetative State.**   True brain death as described in 1.7 is clearly a reason to discontinue all forms of organic support: there are no longer any indications for medical intervention. It must be noted that true brain death is difficult to diagnose in infants; the accepted neurologic criteria for adults are not exactly applicable and must be used with special caution.

Permanent coma or persistent vegetative state also justifies a decision to discontinue medical interventions. Only the goal of sustaining organic life may be accomplished: this is not, in itself, a sufficient justification for continued intervention. The Federal Regulations exempt from treatment "an infant [that] is chronically and irreversibly comatose." [At 14888. In Biblio. Federal Regulations.] However, this clinical diagnosis must be reached with great caution: pediatric neurologists warn that the brains of infants and children may be able to recover even after sustaining serious hypoxic damage.

5.2   **PREFERENCES**

Chapter 2 is entitled Patient Preferences; here the word "patient" is omitted for obvious reasons. However, the preferences of various parties are significant in decisions about the care of infants and children. Among these, the most prominent are the parents of the child. The ethical task is to determine the relevance and weight of parental preferences and how to deal with instances of conflict. Children become capable of expressing their preferences at various ages. When they do, the question arises of how reasonable and relevant these preferences are in matters of medical care.

5.2.1   **Authority of Parents.**   Every child born has biological parents but the authority of parent(s) is a moral, social, and legal matter

It is commonly agreed that parents have the responsibility for the well-being of their children and that they have wide range of discretion to determine in what that well-being will consist. At the same time, parental discretion is not absolute. Infants and children are, in this culture, considered beings in their own right, with certain interests that must be acknowledged regardless of their parent's preferences. Thus, it is usually said that the best interests of the child set limits to the discretion of parents about the upbringing and treatment of their offspring. Also, in this culture, the society as a whole has an interest in the welfare of children and accepts as an obligation the protection of children from harm, even at the hands of their parents.

2.2 **Determination of Parental Responsibility.** In this society, biological parents may have various moral relationships to their offspring. Some have conceived unwillingly and desire to be rid of offspring before or immediately after birth. Others, due to various attitudes or pathologies, have no concern for the child they have borne. Other parties, such as adoptive parents, assume certain responsibilities, perhaps even before legally authorized. Due to shifting social relationships, various adults may undertake moral or legal care of the child at different times. Even if it is possible to determine who bears legal authority, it is not always easy to see who has moral responsibility. Obviously, the greatest weight should be given to those adults who demonstrate emotional attachment and provide support over time. Others, even biological and social parents, might be considered incompetent to make responsible decisions.

2.3 **Parental Incompetence.** Pediatricians and other providers may occasionally suspect parents of serious incompetence in the care of their child. This suspicion must be cautiously evaluated. The most obvious incompetence is revealed by overt and habitual physical abuse of a child. Failure to provide for the ordinary needs of a child represents incompetence due to ignorance, moral turpitude, or certain pathologies, such as addiction. In other cases, failures may be due to inexperience or social conditions. Thus, suspicion of incompetence should be evaluated for its degree, causes, remediability, and so forth. Most importantly, the alleged incompetence should be relevant to the problem at hand. Social workers and others expert at evaluation of social and environmental conditions can be helpful. If suspicions are verified, legal remedies must be sought depending on the seriousness and urgency of the situation. Child protective services exist in every jurisdiction to assist, if this step is necessary.

5.2.4   **Parental Preferences: Standard.**   When parents are properly identified and appear competent as decision makers, they are morally and legally required to observe certain standards in their decision for their child. As the Federal Regulations state, ''The decision to provide or withhold medically indicated treatment is, except in highly unusual circumstances, made by the parents or legal guardians. Parents are the decision makers concerning treatment for their disabled infant, based on the advice and reasonable medical judgment of their physician . . . this role must be respected and supported unless they choose a course of action inconsistent with standards established by law.'' [At 14880. In Biblio. Federal Regulation.] And, it may be added, inconsistent with moral principle. What standards, then, must guide parental choice?

(a) It is clear that medical inefficacy or futility justify a parental decision to discontinue treatment. However, physicians and parents may disagree about the presence of these conditions. Parents may see as inefficacy the failure of a treatment to produce an immediate result or, overcome by the frustration of a long illness, conclude that treatment is futile. It should be noted that inefficacy and futility are intended to represent sound medical judgments and, as such, are in the province of the physician. The physician has the duty to educate the parents, to explain the medical situation, and to strive to achieve a common understanding. If all this fails, and the interventions are, in best medical judgment, inefficacious or futile, the decision to withhold or withdraw them can be made by the physician, who is not obliged to perform action that will not benefit the patient.

It is equally true that physicians may be deluded by their own uncertainty, fear, or therapeutic or scientific zeal, and so fail to recognize or admit that current or proposed interventions are inefficacious or futile. This attitude, which can lead to ethical disasters, must be countered by rigorous honesty, genuine humility, and the willingness to consider the opinions of others.

(b) Every pediatrician must recognize that the birth of a defective infant or the critical illness of a child can be a most traumatic experience for parents. Even the most lucid explanations of the medical problem can be misunderstood. It is difficult for parents to be properly informed and fully consenting proxies. Nevertheless, it is also wrong to depreciate all parents as decision makers on the supposition that no one can make good decisions in a crisis. Each case must be judged on its own. Serious efforts at psychologically and emotionally suitable communication must be made.

(c) If intervention is not clearly inefficacious or futile, decisions should be made in view of the best interests of the infant or child. The phrase, "best interests" will be explained in 5.3. Here it should be noted that the interests of the decision makers, namely, the parents and the physicians, or the interests of society at large are not the central focus: The interests of the patient constitute the standard for decisions made on the behalf of that patient by others.

(d) In cases where differences of opinion between parents and physicians or between parents themselves are irreconcilable, it is necessary to have recourse to the legal system that has been established to protect the welfare of those incapable of protecting themselves. Such resource is often extremely traumatic for all concerned, but it acknowledges that the infant or child, despite its inability to speak for itself, has a valued place in our society.

5.2.5 **Parents with Unusual Beliefs.** Parents are granted wide discretion about the values they believe their children's lives should embody. [2.5.2] Thus, parents may choose the style of their children's education. However, they are not permitted to choose that their children not be educated at all, since such a choice would obviously disadvantage the child's future capabilities. Similarly, parental discretion is limited in medical care when the exercise of certain beliefs would disadvantage the child's health in serious ways.

CASE I. An 11-year-old girl is brought to an ER from an automobile accident. She is unconscious, with shallow, gasping respirations and circumoral cyanosis. Severe contusions are noted across the chest, the left side of which moves paradoxically on inspiration. She is hypotensive and tachycardic. An intravenous infusion of Ringer's lactate is started. After intubation and stabilization of blood pressure, a chest film confirms flail chest and possible pulmonary hemorrhage. Insertion of a chest tube produced frank blood. As the child was being wheeled toward the operating room, the parents, who had arrived mintues before, stepped in front of the gurney and declared that they were Jehovah's Witnesses and refused permission for blood transfusion.

CASE II.   A 10-year-old boy is sent from class to the school nurse complaining of severe headache and malaise. Noting his fever and irritability when moved, the nurse suspects meningitis. She calls the parents who say they will come directly to the school. When they arrive, they introduce themselves as Christian Scientists and the two persons accompanying them as Christian Science Practitioners. They say they will take the child home and ask the nurse not to call the school physician. They remind her that Christian Science Practitioners are considered health professionals by their State Department of Health.

CASE III.   A 13-year-old boy with acute lymphocytic leukemia suffers his second relapse and fails to respond to chemotherapy. Anemic and thrombocytopenic, he understands that transfusion of blood products would make him more comfortable, perhaps even allow him to leave the hospital. He announces that he has been raised as a Jehovah's Witness and refuses transfusions. His parents support his decision.

COMMENT.   Freedom of religion is highly valued. However, it is the freedom of the believer, capable of free and informed adherence to a faith that is valued, not the effects of that belief on others who do not or cannot accept it as their own. As Justice Holmes wrote, "Parents may make martyrs of themselves, but they are not free to make martyrs of their children." It must be noted that neither of the two religious sects mentioned above consider that their children will be damned by medical treatment, nor is there any evidence that they consider their children tainted or excluded from their community.

COUNSEL.   Blood transfusion should be initiated immediately in Case I. Court authority should be obtained if delay will not jeopardize the child; otherwise, authority can be assumed on the basis of innumerable legal precedents allowing treatment in these conditions. In Case II, authority should be sought to bring the child into a medical institution and treatment provided. Every effort should be made to placate the parents and maintain good relations, but the child's well-being, not the parents', is the issue. Case III, however, is different in an important way: the boy is old enough to understand and to have some personal commitments and the prognosis is very poor, even with treatment. Transfusion will not cure, but only palliate. It is ethical to omit transfusion.

5.2.6 **The Preferences of the Child.** As children grow old enough to articulate their preferences and reasons for them, they progressively achieve an entitlement to some respect for these preferences. They are led toward responsible maturity by this respect, as well as by education. However, it is sometimes difficult to decide how much respect to afford to a child's preferences, when these seem to be contrary to the child's welfare. It is also difficult to discern how rational their preferences are, in that consequences and alternatives, as well as relative values, are often not clearly perceived by the child.

CASE I. The same as Case III in 5.2.5.

COMMENT. This boy is making an important decision: he is weighing his own discomfort against a belief he now adheres to with some fervor. The value of the transfusions in achieving significant medical goals is questionable. The boy is aware of his impending death and of the nature of his illness. He even manifests some of those characteristics of responsible decision that we require in adults, even if we might suspect that, if more mature, he would see his beliefs differently. It seems unethical to insist that he subordinate his beliefs for so transitory a benefit.

CASE II. The same as Case II above. Assume that this child is 13 and, when a physician is called, refuses to be seen because he is a Christian Scientist.

COMMENT. The consequences of refusing medical treatment for meningitis are very serious. Even if this youngster was not disoriented due to his illness, it is dubious that he appreciates the dire consequences. It is also uncertain that he appreciates the rather sophisticated doctrine that he professes; a doctrine that does, in fact, allow some forms of medical intervention. Finally, his illness, unlike that of the boy in Case I, is sudden and unexpected. His wishes should not be considered decisive.

> CASE III. The same as Case V in 5.1.3. This girl, who has failed a reasonable course of chemotherapy, might be a candidate for clinical research. She is 7 years old and has had an unhappy experience with previous therapy. Her parents are eager to enter into the trial of a new agent offered by the oncologist. She repeatedly and tearfully refuses.

COMMENT. Therapy and research are significantly different. Therapy promises sound hope of achieving the goal of intervention; research may offer some hope of doing so, but also has as its goal the benefit of other and future patients. A refusal of research by a child, even if it might be thought that the child, if older, would accept, should generally be honored. The National Commission for the Protection of Human Subjects of Biomedical and Behavioral Research [in Biblio.] recommended that age 7 be considered as the point at which a child's consent be sought and refusal honored. This has been criticized as unrealistic, but it emphasizes the point that a child does have the right to refuse interventions that hold more promise for others than for self. [See 4.6 and 5.4.]

In general, the wishes of the maturing child should be seriously considered in decisions about care. Signs that the child has some comprehension of the situation and some appreciation of the consequences should be sought. Solicitous attention should be paid to helping them understand. The influences of fear and distress should be noted. Consultation with persons familiar with the psychology of the maturing child should be sought. Above all, nothing should be done to undermine the trust of the child in the adults who are responsible for care and upbringing.

5.3   **QUALITY OF LIFE**

The general meaning of quality of life, and certain cautions about its relevance to clinical decisions, are noted in Chapter 3. There are some special issues in pediatrics that urge even greater caution. The prefatory remarks to the Federal Regulations warn that "medical treatment decisions are not to be made on the basis of subjective opinions about the future 'quality of life' of a retarded or disabled person.'' [At 14880.] However, the Regulations themselves legitimate some reference to quality of life by allowing permanent coma and the inhumanity of the treatment to serve as justifications for refraining from intervention. Still, the warning does remind us of the danger of discrimination that is fatal for the individuals and unfair to categories of individuals who do not meet certain social norms and standards often quite irrelevant to their medical needs.

5.3.1 **Features of Quality of Life Judgments in Pediatrics.** Two important differences distinguish these judgments from those in adult care. First, the adult often can express preferences about future states of life and health. Second, when an adult is incapable of expressing preferences, the history of that person's preferences and style of life often allows others to estimate how that person would value and adapt to future states. In pediatrics, the life whose quality is being assessed is almost entirely in the future and no expression of preferences is available.

CASE I.   The same as the Example in 5.1.2. A 12-year-old boy with Down's syndrome has a congenital heart lesion. No surgical intervention was recommended until his 12th year. He is now a boy scout, active in sports, and a good performer in special school. His parents refuse permission for surgery that would effect normal longevity, saying that, after they died, his quality of life would be intolerable.

CASE II.   The same as the Example in 5.1.2. A newborn infant is noted to have the stigmata of Down's syndrome, which is confirmed by chromosome studies. He also suffers from duodenal atresia for which immediate surgery is indicated. His parents refuse permission, saying that the baby would be better dead than living the life of a retarded person.

COMMENT.   The perils of quality-of-life judgment are demonstrated in these cases. In Case I, the judgment is about a far future and does not reflect the relative success of this boy in dealing with his limitation. The parents' judgment is not very well founded and has implications of great consequence and certain outcome for their son: deprived of surgical correction, he will continue to live for some time and slowly develop the debilitating effects of severe cardiac insufficiency and pulmonary hypertension. In Case II, a general predisposition to disvalue limited intelligence, achievement, productivity and independence colors judgment. These social values (which are, after all, not the only human values) may be important in our society, but they are not so important that their invocation should lead to death for those who can attain them in only limited degree. The implications of such a position for our social values should be obvious. Questions raised by the social problems of providing appropriate care and education are discussed in 5.4.

COUNSEL. Medical interventions that are generally effective in alleviating the physical disability are ethically mandatory when the only supposed contraindication is mental retardation of the range characteristic of Down syndrome. More complicated medical conditions, such as major cardiac deformity, may be genuine contraindications, but for the same reasons that they may contraindicate surgery for an otherwise normal infant. There is no sound evidence that Down syndrome infants tolerate major surgery any less well than other infants, given current antibiotic therapy.

5.3.2 **Best Interest Standard.** In 5.2.4, decisions made for the patient by proxies, such as parents, were said to be limited to judgments expressing the best interests of the patient. This notion, drawn from legal parlance, is quite vague. Two steps can dispel some of this vagueness. First, what counts as an interest should be designated, as much as possible, from the viewpoint of the one for whom the judgment is being made. The interests common to competent, intelligent persons may not even occur to persons who suffer significant limitations. Still, they have interests in the pursuit and securing of certain values suited to their limitations. The proxy decision makers should attempt to view the world of such persons through their eyes. Second, the interests at stake should be judged by reference to more objective, societally shared values, rather than more individualized values. Thus, in the words of the President's Commission, which advocates use of a best interest standard,

> In assessing whether a procedure or course of treatment would be in a patient's best interests, the surrogate must take into account such fac-

tors as the relief of suffering, the preservation or restoration of functioning, and the quality as well as the extent of life sustained. An accurate assessment will encompass consideration of the satisfaction of present desires, the opportunities for future satisfaction, and the possibility of developing or regaining the capacity for self-determination. [President's Commission for the Study of Ethical Problems in Medicine and Biomedical and Behavioral Research, *Deciding to Forego Life-Sustaining Treatment*, p. 135. (See General References.)]

CASE I.   A full-term infant is noted at birth to have a large thoracolumbar myelomenigocele, which is leaking cerebrospinal fluid. In addition to extreme kyphosis, the infant appears to be microcephalic. Computerized tomography of the head shows cerebral dysgenesis and ventriculomegaly, with a cortical mantle of less than 5 ml. The parents, who understand the situation, request that no medical interventions be performed and that they be allowed to take the infant home to die.

CASE II.   A 1,100 gm. premature male infant, born at 32 weeks gestational age, is now 2 days old and in the recovery phase of moderately severe hyaline membrane disease. A drop in hematocrit and a prolonged indirect hyperbilirubinemia suggest occult bleeding. A cranial ultrasound study confirms a grade III intraventricular hemorrhage. After being informed of the possible risks of mental retardation, the infant's parents request that the mechanical ventilation be stopped.

COMMENT.   In Case I, the prognosis includes severe deformity of the spine and lower limbs, incontinence of bowel and bladder, and the near certainty of profound mental retardation. Multiple surgical procedures will be required during early life for orthopedic problems and there is high likelihood of frequent infection of bladder catheter and ventriculoperitoneal shunt. The child will never be able to understand and communicate about his suffering. The combination of extreme and painful disabilities and severe retardation constitutes a quality of life that can confidently be judged to be undesirable for, and undesired by, any human being.

In Case II, there is a significant probability of retardation, although the extent is unpredictable. There may be some residual chronic lung deficiencies. The difference lies in the predictability, in Case I, of a life of physical pain without even the solace of experiencing the compassion of others and of understanding one's own condition, as contrasted with an uncertain prediction of mental limitation only, in Case II. The judgment of quality of life in the first invokes experiences and states that can confidently be evaluated as those that any human being would wish to avoid.

> NOTE. We describe an extremely bad case of myelodysplasia; today, most experts in the care of this condition recommend early closure of the lesion and continued care for almost all cases. Outcomes have become progressively better over the last decade. There is little sympathy, either among specialists or ethicists for detailed criteria devised to select infants for non-treatment that were popular in the recent past. [See Bibliography 5.3.2.]

COUNSEL.   We propose that a decision to refrain from intervention that is designed to prolong life is ethically justified in Case I, but not in Case II. In our opinion, (although probably not in the opinion of the framers) even the language of the Federal Regulations can be interpreted to support this position: Life-sustaining treatment is not mandatory when "the provision of such treatment would be virtually futile in terms of the survival of the infant and the treatment itself under such circumstances would be inhumane." [At 14888] We are reminded that an obligation of humaneness is as serious as an obligation to save endangered life; humaneness may lead to the judgment that a life of unremitting pain, disability and absence of human communication can be objectively considered unbearable: a life that no person would choose if the choice were given. No moral obligation is imposed on anyone to assist in the perpetuation of such a life in the absence of a request from the one who lives it.

5.3.3(3.3) **Infant Euthanasia.**   Granting the possibility that some decisions to withhold treatment can be ethically justified raises the question whether it may be ethically permissible, even obligatory, to terminate the life of the infant immediately and directly, rather than tolerate a slow, painful death. Some authors see a compelling logic in this position. However, as a matter of practice, it is difficult to accept: it is open to serious abuse and runs counter to the instincts of most persons. It is also legally perilous. Adequate management of pain can be accomplished and measures of comfort instituted.

5.4   **SOCIOECONOMIC FACTORS**

Chapter Four discusses the ethical relevance of benefits and burdens that come to parties other than the patient, as a result of decisions about the patient. In pediatrics, two issues deserve particular notice: the role of the family of the child-patient and the impact on society of certain decisions and policies about care of children.

.4.1   **The Family.**   In 5.2, the nature and scope of parental authority were discussed. The parents of an ill child are often parents of other children and have multiple responsibilities. Decisions about treatment may have major implications for their other children and for the social and financial stability of the family. Often, parents will devote almost exclusive attention to the sick child, but on occasion, they may ask themselves whether this is unfair to themselves and their other children.

> CASE I.   Same as Case I in 5.3.2. The parents of this infant with myelodysplasia have three other children, 12, 8, and 4 years of age. The 8-year-old also had a neural tube defect of lesser severity but developed hydrocephalus, which required shunting, and is also moderately retarded. The family gains its livelihood on a small, unproductive farm and live at some distance from schools and medical facilities. They have been very devoted to the care and education of the 8-year-old and are fearful that the other two children are suffering from the attention given her. They now face the prospect of another handicapped child.

COMMENT.   Counsel in this case recommended that no intervention be provided, in accord with the parent's wishes. However, that counsel was offered in view of the prospects of a life of great pain and suffering for the patient. The welfare of this family and of the other children was not, in itself, the primary justification. Nevertheless, it is an additional consideration that, while not in itself decisive, deserves attention. Had Case II been at stake, a better prognosis would have strongly urged in favor of treatment and the considerations of the family would have been less influential. In making this choice, the possibility that the current patient would be normal or mildly affected means that his presence in the family would not be as disruptive as in the former case.

5.4.2 **Providers' View of Family.**   In 5.2.3, the problem of incompetent parents was noted. Physicians and nurses caring for the sick infant or child may form views of a family that affect their attitude toward treatment. A family of different cultural or socioeconomic status than the providers are accustomed to deal with may bias them against vigorous efforts to save the endangered life. On occasion, the perceived problems may be very real: For example, mother and father are both addicted to drugs and alcohol, live in substandard conditions, and so forth. In other cases, the perception might be quite inaccurate. For example, the family mentioned in 5.4.1 were "mountain people," whose life-style and appearance were quite foreign to the staff of the distant medical center. Yet, they were caring and competent parents who made great sacrifices for their children. Again, appearances may deceive in the other direction. Intelligent and achieving parents, in protecting their social and economic status, may act to the detriment of their child's best interests and, because of their appearance and manner, be tolerated by providers.

COUNSEL.   Acknowledgment of bias is crucial. If problems are genuine and pose a threat to the infant in the home environment, educational means should be employed and, if they fail, legal action initiated through the child protective agency.

5.4.3 **Social Costs of Care.**   The general argument in Chapter 4 is relevant. However, one frequently hears neonatal intensive care singled out as "too costly." On the other hand, the difficulty of obtaining financial and social assistance for many forms of childhood disabilities is sometimes suggested as a justification for a nontreatment decision. These issues are matters of social policy and so lie outside the scope of clinical ethics. However, it must be noted that such considerations do not, of themselves, constitute sufficient grounds for clinical decisions. It is obvious that pediatric medicine, which has a long tradition of concern for the social environments that foster good health, must be deeply involved in the remedy of socioeconomic conditions that pressure parents and physicians toward inappropriate clinical decisions. It is, in our view, an ethical anomaly for government to insist that it has a "compelling interest" in the protection of life and, at the same time, to dismantle the financial and institutional forms that enable good care, education and social support for those whose lives are saved and for their families.

5.4.4   **Organ Transplantation.**   Since successful organ transplantation depends on appropriate immunologic tissue typing, the question may occasionally arise about the taking of a kidney or bone marrow from a healthy child for a seriously ill sibling. This question had an inauspicious answer when first asked, since the healthy child was retarded, thus raising the suspicion that the retarded are to be disvalued and used for the benefit of others. However, the major question is the risk to which a healthy child is put for the possible benefit of another. It seems hardly defensible to impose the serious risks of removal of a kidney, but feasible to suggest the donation of bone marrow. Needless to say, the negotiations with family and with the child require the utmost delicacy, the psychological implications for the children in the event either of failure or success recognized and the legal requirements in the jurisdiction complied with.

5(4.6) **Research.**   The involvement of children as research subjects has been carefully studied by the National Commission for the Protection of Subjects of Biomedical and Behavioral Research [In Biblio.]. The conclusions of that Commission are now embodied in Federal Regulations that reflect sound ethical judgments. In addition to the ethical considerations about research in general, stated in 4.6, pediatric research should be based on the following ethical principles.

(a) There must be sound reasons why the research must be done with children. In general, this will be because the condition under study affects only children and no animal models suffice to study it. The results should be important for the health of children.

(b) The level of risk to the child must be carefully determined. If the risk of the research is nonexistent or minimal, that is, not exceeding the risks allowed children in daily life or the risks of routine medical care, there need be no prospect of benefit to the child to justify the research. If the risks are at all more than minimal, some prospect of personal benefit must be present, that is, the research must also have some therapeutic potential for the subject.

(c) Any research proposal that involves more than minimal risks and offers no personal benefit to the subject requires special review in order to adjudicate its vital importance for the health of children. Institutional review boards, which must approve of all research, can advise researchers about details of the requirements for ethical research involving children.

(d) The permission of parents or guardians, and their close involvement in the research, must be obtained. The consent of the child should also be sought when they are at that stage of maturity where the nature of the procedure and the concept of an invitation to help others voluntarily can be understood. A child's dissent should be respected unless the research procedure is directly associated with a necessary therapy that cannot be provided outside research modalities.

5.4.6 **Public Health.** Vaccination is a major public health measure and is important for the health of individual children. The long effort by pediatricians to institute mandatory or universal immunization is threatened by changes in public health law to permit persons of unusual belief to refuse vaccination and by the growing awareness of parents that vaccination has risks that could lead to serious and possibly uncompensated harm for their children. While this is distressing, the basic principle must be recalled: vaccination does put a child at a small risk of major harm to avoid a somewhat remote threat to its own health in order to contribute to the general safety of other children.

COMMENT. When immunization is compulsory by law, the pediatrician does not obtain "informed consent" (with its counterpart, "informed dissent") from the parents. Rather, full information is given about the necessity for immunization and its risks. If immunization is not compulsory, the pediatrician must respect the parents' wishes, although efforts to educate and persuade are suitable. If parents refuse immunization against a serious disease of epidemic proportions, legal authorization should be sought. The problem of compensation for the harms due to immunization is a matter of social policy. Pediatric medicine should work to ensure the establishment of an equitable system for compensation of those who are involuntarily exposed to risks for the public good.

BIBLIOGRAPHY

5.1 *Pediatric Ethics*

Coburn, R. Morality and the defective newborn. J Med Philos, 1980, 5: 340.

Committee on Bioethics. Treatment of critically ill newborns. Pediatrics, 1983, 72:565-566.

Coplan, J. Wrongful life and wrongful birth: New concepts for the pediatrician. Pediatrics, 1985, 75:65.

Duff, R., Campbell, A. G. Moral and ethical dilemmas in the special care nursery. N Engl J Med, 1973, 289:890.

Holder, A. *Legal Issues in Pediatrics and Adolescent Medicine*. New York: John Wiley & Sons, 1977.

Jonsen, A. Justice and the defective newborn. In *Justice and Health Care*. E. Shelp (ed). Boston: D. Reidel, 1981.

Jonsen, A., Phibbs, R., Tooley, W., Garland, M. Critical issues in newborn intensive care. Pediatrics, 1975, 55:756.

Lyon, J. *Playing God in the Nursery*. New York: Norton, 1985.

Murray, T. The final anticlimactic rule on Baby Doe. Hastings Cent Rep, 1985, 15(3):5.

Murray, T., Caplan, A. *Which Babies Shall Live? Humanistic Implications of the Care of Imperiled Newborns*. Clifton, N.J.: Humana Press, 1985.

Robertson, J., Fost, N. Passive euthanasia of defective newborn infants: Legal considerations. J Pediatr, 1976, 88:883.

Schwartz, J., Baxter, J., Brill, D., et al. Diagnosis of brain death. Pediatrics, 1984, 73:14.

Sherlock, R. Selective non-treatment of newborns, J Med Ethics, 1979, 5:139.

Weber, L. *Who Shall Live? The Dilemma of the Severely Handicapped Child*. New York: Paulist Press, 1976.

Wier, R. *Selective Treatment of Handicapped Newborns*. New York: Oxford University Press, 1984.

5.2 *Preferences*

Ackerman, T. F. The limits of beneficence: Jehovah's Witnesses and childhood cancer. Hastings Cent Rep, 1980, 10(4):13.

Fost, N. Parental control over children. Pediatrics, 1983, 103:571.

Fost, N. The rights of emotionally abused children. Pediatrics, 1982, 101:215.

Fost, N. Counseling families who have a child with severe congenital anomalies. Pediatrics, 1981, 67:321.

Gaylin, W., Macklin, R. (eds). *Who Speaks for the Child? The Problem of Proxy Consent*. New York: Plenum, 1982.

Hofmann, A. D. Consent and confidentiality: Their legal and ethical implications for adolescent medicine. In *Medical Care of the Adolescent* (3rd ed.). J. R. Gallagher, F. P. Heald, D. C. Garell (eds). New York: Appleton-Centry-Crofts, 1976, pp. 42–56.

Holder, A. Parents, courts and refusal of treatment. Pediatrics, 1983, 103:515.

Leiken, S. Minors' assent or dissent to medical treatment. Pediatrics, 1983, 102:169.

Nitschke, R., Humphrey, G., Sexauer, C., et al. Therapeutic choices by patients with end stage cancer. Pediatrics, 1982, 101:471.

Shaw, A. Dilemmas of "informed consent" in children. N Engl J Med, 1973, 289:973.

Swan, R. Faith healing, Christian Science and the medical care of children. N Engl J Med, 1983, 309:1639.

Shelp, E. *Born to Die*. New York: The Free Press, 1986.

Talbot, N.A. The position of the Christian Science Church. N Engl J Med, 1983, 309:1641.

Todres, I., Krane, D., Howell, M., et al. Pediatricians' attitudes affecting decision making in defective newborns. Pediatrics, 1977, 60:197.

5.3 *Quality of Life*

Fletcher, J. Abortion, euthanasia, and care of defective newborns. N Engl J Med, 1975, 292:75.

Freeman, J. To treat or not to treat: Ethical dilemmas of treating the infant with myelomenigocele. Clin Neurosurg, 1973, 20:134.

Goldstein, J., Freud, A., Solnit, A. *Before the Best Interests of the Child*. New York: Free Press, 1980.

Gustafson, J. Mongolism, parental desires, and the right to life. Perspec Biol Med, 1973, 16(4):529.

Kohl, M. (ed). *Infanticide and the Value of Life*. Buffalo, NY: Prometheus, 1978.

Lorber, J. Ethical problems in the management of myelomeningocele and hydrocephalus. J R Coll Phys, 1975, 10(1):47.

McCormick, R. To save or let die. JAMA, 1974, 229:172.

Silverman, W. A. Hospice setting for humane neonatal death. Pediatrics, 1982, 69:239.

Singer, P. Sanctity of life or quality of life? Pediatrics, 1983, 72:128.

Smith, G., et al. The rights of infants with Down's syndrome. JAMA, 1984, 251:229.

Swinyard, C. (ed). *Decision Making and the Defective Newborn*. Springfield, Ill. Charles C. Thomas, 1978.

Veatch, R. The technical criteria fallacy. Hastings Cent Rep, 1977, 7(4):15.

5.4 *Socioeconomic Factors*

Jonsen, A. Research involving children. Pediatrics, 1978, 62:131.

Miller, C. The health of children, a crisis of ethics. Pediatrics, 1984, 73:550.

National Commission for Protection of Human Subjects of Biomedical and Behavioral Research. *Research Involving Children*, Washington, D.C.: U.S. Government Printing Office, 1977.

Sinclair, J., et al. Evaluation of neonatal intensive care programs. N Engl J Med, 1981, 305:489.

Stahlman, N. T. Newborn intensive care: Success or failure? Pediatrics, 1984, 105:162–167.

GENERAL
REFERENCES

Resources

BioethicsLine. National Library of Medicine Data Base. Medlars Management National Library of Medicine. 8600 Rockville Pike, Bethesda, Md. 20209.

Duncan, A. S. *Dictionary of Medical Ethics*. New York: Crossroads, 1981.

Hastings Center's Bibliography of Ethics, Biomedicine and Professional Responsibility. University Publications of America. 44 North Market, Frederick, Md. 21701, issued biannually.

President's Commission for the Study of Ethical Problems in Medicine and Biomedical and Behavioral Research. *Defining Death. A Report on the Medical, Legal and Ethical Issues in the Determination of Death*. Washington, D.C.: Government Printing Office, 1981.

President's Commission for the Study of Ethical Problems in Medicine and Biomedical and Behavioral Research. *Making Health Care Decisions. A Report on the Ethical and Legal Implications of Informed Consent in the Patient–Practitioner Relationship*. Washington, D.C.: Government Printing Office, 1982.

President's Commission for the Study of Ethical Problems in Medicine and Biomedical and Behavioral Research. *Deciding to Forego Life-*

Sustaining Treatment. A Report on the Ethical, Medical, and Legal Issues in Treatment Decisions. Washington, D.C.: Government Printing Office, 1983.

President's Commission for the Study of Ethical Problems in Medicine and Biomedical and Behavioral Research. *Securing Access to Health Care. The Ethical Implications of Differences in the Availability of Health Services.* Washington D.C.: Government Printing Office, 1983.

Reich, W. (ed). *Encyclopedia of Bioethics.* 2 vols. New York: Free Press, 1982.

Walters, L., Kahn, T. *Bibliography of Bioethics.* The Kennedy Institute of Ethics. Georgetown University, Washington, D.C. 20057, issued annually.

Journals

The principal journals devoted exclusively or in large part to medical ethics are:

Hastings Center Report. Institute of Society, Ethics and the Life Sciences. 360 Broadway, Hastings-on-Hudson, N.Y. 10706.

Journal of Medical Ethics. Society for the Study of Medical Ethics. Tavistock House East. Tavistock Sq., London, WCIH 9JR.

Journal of Medicine and Philosophy. Boston: D. Reidel.

Journal of Theoretical Medicine. Boston: D. Reidel.

Linacre Quarterly. A Journal of the Philosophy and Ethics of Medical Practice. The National Federation of Catholic Physicians' Guilds. 850 Elm Grove Road, Elm Grove, Wis. 53122.

Anthologies and Collected Essays

Abrams, N., Buckner, M. *Medical Ethics. A Clinical Textbook and Reference for Health Care Professionals.* Cambridge, Mass.: MIT Press, 1983.

Abernethy, V. (ed). *Frontiers in Medical Ethics: Applications in a Medical Setting.* Cambridge, Mass.: Ballinger, 1980.

Bayles, M. B., High, D. M. (eds). *Medical Treatment of the Dying: Moral Issues.* Cambridge, Mass.: Henkman, 1978.

Beauchamp, T. L., Walters, L. (eds). *Contemporary Issues in Bioethics, 2nd Ed.,* Encino, Calif.: Dickenson Publishing Co., 1982.

Cassell, E., Siegler, M. *Changing Values in Medicine.* Frederick, Md.: University Publications of America, 1985.

Gorovitz, S., Macklin, R., Jameton, A. *Moral Problems in Medicine, 2nd Ed.,* Englewood Cliffs, N.J.: Prentice-Hall, 1983.

Horan, D. J., Mall, D. *Death, Dying and Euthanasia.* Washington D.C.: University Publications of America, 1977.

Humber, J. M., Almeder, R. F. (eds). *Biomedical Ethics and the Law.* New York: Plenum, 1976.

Hunt, R., Arras, J. (eds). *Ethical Issues in Modern Medicine*. Palo Alto, Calif.: Mayfield, 1979.

Ladd, J. (ed). *Ethical Issues Relating to Life and Death*. New York: Oxford University Press, 1979.

New England Journal of Medicine. *Clinical Medical Ethics*. (reprinted collection of 22 articles) 1985.

Reiser, S. J., Dyke, A. J., Curran, W. J. (eds). *Ethics in Medicine: Historical Perspectives and Contemporary Concerns*. Cambridge, Mass.: MIT Press, 1977.

Robison, W. L., Pritchard, M. S. (eds). *Medical Responsibility*. Clifton, N.J.: Humana Press, 1979.

Siegler, M. (ed). *Paying the Price of Medical Progress*. Ann Arbor: University of Michigan/Health Administration Press, 1986.

Shannon, T. A. (ed). *Bioethics*. New York: Paulist Press, 1976.

Williams, R. H. (ed). *To Live and to Die: When, Why, and How*. New York: Springer, 1974.

General Works and Texts

Beauchamp, T. L., Childress, J. F. *Principles of Biomedical Ethics*. New York: Oxford University Press, 1979.

Beauchamp, T. L., McCullough, L. B. *The Moral Responsibilities of Physicians*. Englewood Cliffs, N.J.: Prentice-Hall, 1984.

Bliss, B. P., Johnson, A.G. *Aims and Motives in Clinical Medicine*. London: Beckman, 1975.

Brody, H. *Ethical Decisions in Medicine*. 2nd ed. Boston: Little, Brown, 1981.

Campbell, A. *Moral Dilemmas in Medicine*. Baltimore: Williams & Wilkins, 1972.

Fletcher, J. *Humanhood: Essays in Biomedical Ethics*. Buffalo, N.Y.: Prometheus Books, 1979.

Fletcher, J. *Morals and Medicine*. Boston: Little, Brown, 1960.

Francoeur, R. *Biomedical Ethics*. New York: Wiley, 1983.

Graber, G., Beasley, A., Eaddy, J. *Ethical Analysis of Clinical Medicine*. Baltimore: Urban and Schwarzenberg, 1985.

Meyers, D. *Medicolegal Implications of Death and Dying*. San Francisco: Bancroft-Whitney, 1981 (with annual supplements).

Munson, R. *Intervention and Reflection: Basic Issues in Medical Ethics*. Belmont, Calif.: Wadsworth Publishing Co., 1979.

Pellegrino, E. O., Thomasna, D. C. *A Philosophical Basis of Medical Ethics*. New York: Oxford University Press, 1981.

Ramsey, P. *Patient as Person*. New Haven, Conn.: Yale University Press, 1970.

Smith, H. L. *Ethics and the New Medicine*. Nashville, Tenn.: Abingdon, 1970.

Vaux, K. *Biomedical Ethics: Morality for the New Medicine*. New York: Harper & Row, 1974.

Veatch, R. M. *A Theory of Medical Ethics*. New York: Basic Books, 1981.

Veatch, R. M. *Case Studies in Medical Ethics*. Cambridge, Mass.: Harvard University Press, 1977.

Warner, R. *Morality in Medicine*. Sherman Oaks, Calif.: Alfred Publishing, 1980.

Winslade, W., Ross, J. *Choosing Life or Death*. New York: The Free Press, 1986.

Books and Resources in the Roman Catholic Tradition

Ashley, B. M., O'Rourke, K. D. *Health Care Ethics: A Theological Analysis*. St. Louis: Catholic Hospital Assoc., 1978.

Healy, E. *Medical Ethics*. Chicago: Loyola University Press, 1956.

Kelly, G. *Medico-Moral Problems*. St. Louis: Catholic Hospital Association, 1953.

McCarthy, D., Moraczewski, A. (eds). *Moral Responsibility in Prolonging Life*. St. Louis: Pope John XIII Center, 1981.

McFadden, C. J. *Medical Ethics*. Philadelphia: Davis, 1967.

O'Donnell, T. J. *Morals in Medicine*. Washington, D.C.: Newman Press, 1957.

United States Catholic Conference. *Ethical and Religious Directives for Catholic Health Facilities*. Washington: United States Catholic Conference, 1971.

Books and Resources in the Jewish Tradition

Bleich, B. *Judiasm and Healing*. New York: KTAV Publishing, 1980.

Gribetz, D., Tendler, M. (eds). Medical ethics: The Jewish Point of View. Mt. Sinai J Med, 1984, 51:1.

Jakobovits, I. *Jewish Medical Ethics*. New York: Yeshiva University Press, 1972.

Medical Ethics from the Jewish Perspective. J Med Philos, 1983:8; 1.

Rosner, F. *Modern Medicine and Jewish Law*. New York: Yeshiva University Press, 1972.

Rosner, F., Bleich, B. *Jewish Bioethics*. New York: Sanhedrin Press, 1979.

Tendler, M. *Medical Ethics: A Compendium of Jewish Moral, Ethical and Religious Principles in Medical Practice*. New York: Committee on Religious Affairs of the Federation of Jewish Philanthropies, 1975.